The

HERITAGE
BOOK

1 9 9 6

The

HERITAGE
BOOK
1 9 9 6

Edna McCann

Prentice Hall Canada Inc.
Scarborough, Ontario

© 1996 Prentice-Hall Canada Inc., Scarborough, Ontario

Prentice-Hall, Inc., Englewood Cliffs, New Jersey
Prentice-Hall International (UK) Limited, London
Prentice-Hall of Australia, Pty. Limited, Sydney
Prentice-Hall Hispanoamericana, S.A., Mexico City
Prentice-Hall of India Private Limited, New Delhi
Prentice-Hall of Japan, Inc., Tokyo
Simon & Schuster Asia Private Limited, Singapore
Editora Prentice-Hall do Brasil, Ltda., Rio de Janeiro

ISBN 0-13-220682-X

Copy Editor: Karen Rolfe
Production Editor: Kelly Dickson
Production Coordinator: Anita Boyle-Evans
Page Layout: Joan Morrison

1 2 3 4 5   F   00 99 98 97 96

Printed and bound in Canada

PICTURE CREDITS

Winter
  Gord Handley
  Charlene Daley
  Gord Handley
  Charlene Daley
  Charlene Daley
  Gord Handley
  Charlene Daley
  Florence Gillespie

Summer
  Charlene Daley
  Charlene Daley
  Charlene Daley
  Charlene Daley
  Charlene Daley
  Charlene Daley
  Gord Handley
  Gord Handley

Spring
  Gord Handley
  Gord Handley
  Charlene Daley
  Vince Farr
  Gord Handley
  Gord Handley
  Florence Gillespie
  Gord Handley

Autumn
  Gord Handley
  Gord Handley
  Gord Handley
  Charlene Daley
  Vince Farr
  Gord Handley
  Gord Handley
  Charlene Daley

Introduction

There is so much beauty in the world that you needn't go far to find it. I see it everywhere: in sunlight on water, in the laughter of children, in a handful of daisies, and in smiling faces around the family table. Yes—it's the little things that bring us joy.

It's hard to believe that this is the twentieth year for *The Heritage Book*. Looking back over the years, I take true delight in recalling the experiences and the people who have inspired me as I have prepared these collections. With each new volume, I feel closer to my readers, and I hope it brings us all closer to our loved ones and our communities.

A heartfelt thank-you to all of my readers—*you* are the ones who make my work such a pleasure, and I hope that the 1996 edition of *The Heritage Book* brings you many treasured moments.

Edna McCann

January

Monday January 1

Eleanor Farjeon wrote "A Wish" to celebrate the new year.

A glad New Year to all!—
Since many a tear
Do what we can, must fall,
The greater need to wish a glad New Year!

Since lovely youth is brief,
O girl and boy,
And no one can escape a share of grief
I wish you joy;

Since hate is with us still,
I wish men love;
I wish, since hovering hawks still strike to kill,
The coming of the dove;

And since the ghouls of terror and despair
Are still abroad,
I wish the world once more within the care
Of those who have seen God.

My wish for you, dear readers is a happy and healthy year to enjoy to the fullest measure.

Tuesday January 2

LORD, where we are wrong, make us willing to change; where we are right, make us easy to live with.

Rev. Peter Marshall

Wednesday January 3

As WE move into this year, 1996, I am astounded that another year has passed by so quickly. I know it sounds trite but I don't know where the time goes. It seems as if only last week that we were welcoming 1995 and yet here we are at the beginning of 1996.

My son-in-law Bruce made several New Year's resolutions, the first being to lose weight and the second to relax and enjoy life a little more.

This evening when he came home he was laughing to himself "Marg, Mother—wait until you see this. I am always saying 'Time passes so quickly.' Well in my desk today I found my New Year's resolutions for the past 5 years and guess what! Every one of them started with 'Lose weight' and 'Relax and enjoy life.' I think this had better be the year I stick to them!"

Ah yes—time flies.

Thursday January 4

A T THE bottom of all the tributes paid to democracy is the little man walking into the little booth with a little pencil, making a little cross on a little bit of paper. No amount of rhetoric or voluminous discussion can possibly diminish the overwhelming importance of that point.

Winston Churchill

Friday January 5

O UR creator would never have made such lovely days, and have given us the deep hearts to enjoy them, above and beyond all thought, unless we were meant to be immortal.

Nathaniel Hawthorne

Saturday January 6

TODAY IS THE CELEBRATION OF THE EPIPHANY.

" A ND lo the star which they saw in the east went before them, till it came and stood over where the young child was. When they saw the star, they rejoiced with exceeding great joy. And when they were come into the house, they saw the young child with Mary, his mother, and fell down and worshipped him."

Matthew 2:9–11

Sunday January 7

D o not judge lest you be judged. For in the way you judge, you will be judged, and by your standard of measure, it will be measured to you.

Matthew 7:1–2

Monday January 8

I GREATLY enjoyed the company of my friend Jake Frampton at dinner this evening.

Jake is one of those rare dear friends with whom one feels entirely comfortable in all situations.

"I don't mind telling you Edna, that I'm quite glad that the holiday season has passed. It isn't that I don't love my family dearly but having them with me for a whole week is almost more than I can stand. I guess I've been on my own so long and I am now pretty set in my ways so that having people in my kitchen disrupting my cupboards is downright annoying.

Gosh, listen to me—pretty soon people will start calling me 'Scrooge!'"

For all of his blustering, I'm sure Jake enjoyed the holiday season and will invite them all back again next year.

Tuesday January 9

A FRIEND of mine has recently embarked on a most remarkable experience. She has left on the *S.S. Universe* for a "Seminar at Sea" in the Caribbean.

"The ship was originally purchased in 1971 by Hong Kong shipping magnate and philanthropist C.Y. Tung to provide undergraduate students with an opportunity to transform classroom and international field studies into a global cross-cultural experience.

The ship carries 550 passengers and has numerous classrooms and a superb university library.

Now youthful and mature students alike are learning together hoping to promote peace through understanding.

"Semesters at Sea" are 100-day round-the-world voyages offered every spring and fall. These trips attract renowned professors in every field of study and "Semester at Sea" is a well-respected program given full credit by many universities.

For us older folks who might find it too much to spend three months in the company of so many young people, this two-week "Seminar at Sea" is perfect. There are six Caribbean ports of call and five university professors on board to give theme lectures. Edna, I am so excited!"

What a wonderful experience.

Wednesday January 10

'TIS winter, yet there is no sound along the air
Of winds and their battle-ground; but gently there
The snow is falling—all around.

Ralph Hoyt

Thursday January 11

EVERY life has its dark and cheerful hours. Your level of happiness comes from choosing which to remember.

Friday January 12

LET every dawn of the morning be to you as the beginning of life. And let the setting of the sun be to you as its close. Then let everyone of these short lives leave its sure record of some kindly thing done for others; some good strength or knowledge gained for yourself.

John Ruskin

Saturday January 13

ALTHOUGH I was not always a cat fancier I have become quite fond of my great-granddaughter's little kitten "Kitty." This poem "On a Cat Ageing" by Alexander Gray is for all of my readers who are cat lovers.

He blinks upon the hearth-rug
And yawns in deep content,
Accepting all the comforts
That providence has sent.

Louder he purrs, and louder,
In one glad hymn of praise
For all the night's adventures,
For quiet, restful days.

Life will go on forever,
With all that cat can wish;
Warmth, and the glad procession
Of fish and milk and fish.

Only—the thought disturbs him—
He's noticed once or twice,
That times are somehow breeding
A nimbler race of mice.

Sunday January 14

L ET the words of my mouth, and the meditation of my heart, be acceptable in Thy sight, O Lord, my strength, and my redeemer.

Psalm 19:14

Monday January 15

M Y daughter Margaret and I spent a most enjoyable weekend working on something very special.

A short time ago Marg found in our local bookstore, a mother's memory book *To My Daughter, With Love*. She purchased three of these books, one for me to work on for her, her own, to give to Phyllis, and one for Phyllis to do for Jenny. There are three parts to the book—about my mother, about myself, and about my daughter. Under each of these headings there are pages to write on, such things as "my earliest memories of her," "life in my mother's day," and "my happiest memories of her." "About myself"—our house and street, my first romance, love and marriage— are just a few of the topics to recall and then there are pages to write recollections "about my daughter."

Marg and I really loved comparing notes and I know Phyllis will have her own recollections for her daughter's book.

—Ah memories—

Tuesday January 16

MARTIN Luther King, American clergyman and civil rights leader, would have been 67 years old yesterday.

Assassinated in the prime of his life, he left us with a wonderful legacy—that of the non-violent struggle for change.

I'm sure that, were he alive today, he would be very proud to know that he had such a profound effect on the struggle for equality for his race.

"Free at last, free at last...."

Wednesday January 17

MY good friends Will and Muriel stopped by today and as usual they had stories to tell of their grandchildren.

"You know Edna, Will has come up with a terrific new way to entertain the grandkids when they visit. Some months ago we bought a new mattress and box spring but Will, ever a pack rat, saved our old set.

Now when the kids come over Will gets out their 'trampoline' and they are happy for hours."

Thursday January 18

I HAD a lovely visit today with my friend and neighbour Lila MacGuiness. She served a delicious rhubarb coffee cake and she shared the recipe with me. I'm sure you will find it as delicious as I did.

1/2 cup butter or margarine
1 1/2 cups granulated sugar
2 eggs
1 cup sour cream
1 tsp. vanilla
2 cups all purpose flour
1 tsp baking soda
2 cups finely cut rhubarb

Topping
1/2 cup brown sugar
1 tbsp. all purpose flour
1 tsp. cinnamon
1 tbsp. butter or margarine

Cream butter and sugar. Beat in eggs, one at a time. Stir in sour cream and vanilla. Fold flour and baking soda into the batter. Stir in rhubarb. Turn into a greased 9" x 13" pan. Mix topping ingredients until crumbly. Sprinkle over batter. Bake in a preheated 350° oven for 30–40 minutes.

Friday January 19

THE key to success is perseverance. Sir Lawrence Olivier began his distinguished acting career with a small part as a police officer. In his first appearance on stage, he tripped over a piece of the scenery and fell into the footlights.

Thankfully he overcame this inauspicious beginning and went on to become one of the world's finest and most beloved actors.

Saturday January 20

I DO not believe there is a problem in this country or the world today which could not be settled if approached through the teaching of the "Sermon on the Mount."

Harry S. Truman

Sunday January 21

AN EVENING PRAYER:

LIGHTEN our darkness, we beseech thee, O Lord; and by thy great mercy defend us from all perils and dangers of this night; for the love of thy only Son, our Savour Jesus Christ. Amen.

The Book of Common Prayer

Monday January 22

M Y daughter Julia returned from a recent visit to the U.S.A. and brought back a catalogue from L.L. Bean, the American clothing company.

As we sat together admiring woollen sweaters, corduroy pants and the like, memories came flooding back.

When I was young my parents would always get the Eaton's catalogue and we children would pore over it hour after hour selecting the wonderful things that we would buy "when we get rich."

Very often mother would order such unexciting things as underwear or a new roasting pan— but even these mundane things took on a greater importance when the mailman would announce "Parcel for you at the Post Office."

We would rush down to collect the parcel knowing that, often, there would be some small "surprise" for each of us.

Usually our treat would be some inexpensive toy but it was always enough to satisfy our craving for "store-bought" items—true luxuries in a preacher's home.

Tuesday January 23

M Y son-in-law John is a minister and I always enjoy hearing church anecdotes. "A petite young woman who was about to preach her first sermon began with 'If anyone at the back can't hear me, please let me know.'

The congregation laughed when a voice from the rear spoke out 'I can hear you just fine—but where are you?'"

Wednesday January 24

B ECAUSE perseverance is so difficult, even when supported by the grace of God, thence is the value of new beginnings. For new beginnings are the life of perseverance.

Rev. E.B. Pusey

Thursday January 25

T RY to do unto others as you would have them do to you, and do not be discouraged if they fail sometimes. It is much better that they should fail than that you should.

Charles Dickens

Friday January 26

Bruce and Marg enjoyed a fund-raising dance for our local Lions Club this evening. Although Bruce is not a Lion member himself, he and Marg often join friends in supporting this worthwhile organization.

The Lions Club is the youngest service organization, founded in 1917 in Chicago by an insurance salesman named Melvin Jones. His ideal was to provide service to his fellow men without regard to politics, religion, race or the personal interests of the members. The name Lions comes from Liberty, Intelligence, Our Nation's Safety.

The International Association has grown over the years and now embraces more than 1.5 million members in 177 countries worldwide.

All monies raised from the public by a Lions Club must be returned to the community and other worthwhile causes, while the costs of operating the Clubs, the District, the International Office, as well as the running of conventions etc. come exclusively from the Lions themselves.

The Lions Club in our area is extremely active and the men and women involved add much to the life of our community.

Saturday January 27

WHEN you feel discouraged and most like giving up—don't!

Sunday January 28

IF I take the wings of the morning and dwell in the uttermost parts of the sea; even there shall Thy hand lead me, and Thy right hand shall hold me.

Psalm 139:9–10

Monday January 29

As a lawyer, my grandson Marshall does some work that is involved with real estate. A friend of his recently gave him a letter with "updated key-phrase translations" of real estate advertisement jargon.

Sophisticated city living—Beside (or above) an all-night bar.
Updated kitchen—The sink no longer leaks.
Security system—Neighbour owns an attack dog.
Needs T.L.C.—A disaster, move in at your own risk.
Convenient—Located on a highway entrance ramp.
Cozy—No room is larger than 9' x 6'.
Motivated seller—Has been on the market for 7 years.

Tuesday January 30

L ET the moonbeams cast their shadows
On the snow-clad earth tonight,
We will bind our family closer
By the cozy fireplace light.

I can think of nothing more pleasant on a cold winter's night than a warm fire, a cup of tea and a good book to read.

This evening I am lucky enough to have all three of those things and I plan to take full advantage of my good fortune.

I hope that wherever you are your evening will be pleasantly passed enjoying your many blessings.

Wednesday January 31

H ERE is good advice for a happy marriage: Try to treat your mate in such a fashion that if you should die it would take more than an electric blanket to replace you.

The Radiant Quest

February

Thursday February 1

WALK a mile in the winter twilight, Mark its
whiteness and breathe its cold, Reach your
hand to the sunset embers,
Warm them there, and when you are old
There will be times when you recall it;
A beautiful, perfect shining while,
That will glow in your heart like a splendid
diamond—
You will remember that winter mile.

You will recall the clean cold stinging
Of winter wind on your throat and lips;
The lift of your heart in its youthful gladness,
The tingle of blood to your fingertips;
You will have drawn to your heart forever
This hour, the snow, the light in the west—
Walk awhile in the winter twilight,
Store its treasures within your breast.

Grace Noll Crowell

Friday February 2

Today is the day when many of us eagerly await the weather report from "Wiarton Willie," the weather-predicting groundhog. Should Willie see his shadow as he emerges from his hole we may expect six more weeks of winter-like weather.

Many people doubted the accuracy of this small seer but back in 1994 he correctly predicted a continuation of winter and we were not disappointed. In fact, we endured one of the longest and coldest winters on record.

So it is with great trepidation that I listen to hear today's report. I am ready for spring—already.

Saturday February 3

I am tired of hearing about self-made men. There is not a self-made man in the world. The so-called self-made man is the man who has seized his opportunities, and those given him by circumstances, and has made use of them.

Lucius Tuttle

Sunday February 4

In all thy ways acknowledge Him, and He shall direct thy paths.

Proverbs 3:6

Monday February 5

O NE of the more unpleasant aspects of the winter weather is the cold that I seem to catch each year in spite of my best efforts to avoid it.

When you have a cold, however, you are never short of friends with good ideas about chasing it away.

Here are just a few of the helpful tips that I have received over the past few days.

1. Buy the most effective over-the-counter antihistamine. According to studies the antihistamine that works best in fighting the runny nose and watery eyes of a cold is chlorpheniramine so the product that you buy should have this listed on the formula label.
2. Sometimes an anti-inflammatory drug, such as those used to treat arthritis, may ease cold symptoms—particularly cough and headache. Naprosyn is recommended by many researchers.
3. Natural cures, usually my favourites, should include the taking of plenty of fluids, to help ease congestion, relieve respiratory irritation, and soothe sore throats.

As well, chicken soup—with vegetables—somewhat reduces the inflammation-producing activity of white blood cells.

Of course vitamin C has long been considered therapy for a cold.

With these remedies your cold should disappear in 2 weeks. Left completely alone it could take 14 days!

Tuesday February 6

LIFE is either a daring adventure or nothing. To keep our faces toward change and behave like free spirits in the presence of fate is strength undefeatable.

Helen Keller

Wednesday February 7

EVERY area of trouble gives out a ray of hope, and the one unchangeable certainty is that nothing is certain or unchangeable.

John F. Kennedy

Thursday February 8

GENERAL principles are not the less true or important because from their nature they elude immediate observation; they are like the air, which is not the less necessary because we neither see nor feel it.

William Hazlett

Friday February 9

THE severe cold and wintery weather is especially hard on us seniors. Predictably it is even more difficult for the shut-ins or residents of nursing homes who cannot get out during these days of harsh weather.

Marg and I do our best to spend time regularly at our local nursing home and during a recent visit I had a chance to read this poem, which certainly points out the importance of visitors.

My aged head lifts and turns toward the hall
Could it be that someone is paying me a call?
Footsteps draw near, hope stirs anew
Who could it be? Friends left are so few.
A strand of loose hair is tucked quickly in place
My dress is smoothed out; steps slow in pace.
A woman comes in; the room fills with perfume
"Oh I'm sorry...I have the wrong room."

"Miss Stone, do you know her?" "Yes dear, in
   room four."
Slightly embarrassed, she goes out the door.
My tired heart aches, hands grip the chair;
The clock seems to tick..."no one to care."
Christmas and Easter people come through
Distributing gifts, handmade and new.
Then, soon forgotten, until the next year;
No one remembers that I reside here.
Patients pass on. Then daughters and sons
Say in the halls "I did mean to come."
Dear God...Dear God...Please let it be
That one will remember and come visit me.

Eleanor Beakley

Saturday February 10

M Y friend Emily winters in the sunny south. In
a recent letter she wrote to me of a most
interesting story from Blountstown, Florida.

Betsy Knight and a team of volunteers care for
abandoned, orphaned or injured wildlife, and in
recent years one of the rooms in her home has
been the headquarters of the Big Bend Wildlife
Sanctuary.

In 30 years of caring for wildlife she has cared
for hummingbirds, eagles, reptiles, bats and now
bears.

In 1985 a wildlife officer brought Betsy her first pair of orphaned bear cubs. Soon after she became the only woman sanctioned by the state to raise bears.

The young cubs are cuddled, bottle-fed and burped until they are weaned at the age of 3 months. Then she must avoid touching them as bears attach to humans easily and the ultimate aim is to return them to the wild.

To these bears she is not human she is Mama.

How lucky it is that there are people in this world so caring.

Sunday February 11

B LESSED be the Lord, who daily bears our burden, the God who is our salvation.

Psalm 69:19

Monday February 12

W HEN you judge others you are revealing your own fears and prejudices.

Tuesday February 13

A CTION may not always bring happiness; but there is no happiness without action.

Benjamin Disraeli

Wednesday February 14

VALENTINE'S DAY

Today is that special day of the year when we do something out of the ordinary for our loved ones.

One of the most wonderful Valentine's Days that I remember came early in our marriage. We had just moved into a new parish with our three young daughters and money (or lack thereof) was an ever-present worry.

One of the members of our church turned up at our home with a dinner for the family. Turkey, mashed potatoes, gravy, vegetables, dessert, even candles in silver candlesticks were set upon our table with a card reading—"A Valentine welcome to you all."

I have never forgotten that kindness in all these years.

Thursday February 15

Business underlies everything in our national life, including our spiritual life. Witness the fact that in the Lord's Prayer the first petition is for daily bread. No one can worship God or love his neighbour on an empty stomach.

Woodrow Wilson

Friday February 16

MY granddaughter Phyllis has a friend, Christie, who is a teacher. Christie told Phyllis this amusing story.

"Each year during the winter months there are usually one or two days where the weather is so bad that schools are closed and we get a "snow day" holiday.

During a particularly trying week I woke up about 6:00 a.m. and turned on the radio to hear 'Last night's vicious snow storm has dumped enormous amounts of snow in our area and it looks as if there'll be a number of closures.'

I was so excited to think that I didn't have to get up! Then as I listened I heard 'All Charleston schools are closed, as are U. Mass., Lowell and B.U.'

Somehow my radio was picking up a Boston radio station!

I had to get up and go to school. How disappointing."

Saturday February 17

TODAY as I was going through some boxes of old papers I was surprised to find a small card printed by the Canadian Reconstruction Association on March 1, 1920. On this card were printed "Ten Commandments for Canadian Trade." After you have read them try to think about what still applies in 1996, seventy-six years later.

1. Buy Canadian Products—in doing so you develop the home market, encourage factory expansion and provide employment for new populations and create bigger and better markets for all kinds of farm produce.
2. Import only necessities, and then only if similar Canadian articles or substitutes are not available.
3. Produce to the limit in field and factory.
4. Cooperate, conserve, specialize, standardize.
5. Develop export markets. Foreign business gives stability to trade.
6. Utilize Canadian services.
7. Manufacture raw materials.
8. Use science for the determination and development of natural resources.
9. Make quality the hallmark of Canadian products.

10. Be fair to capital. Canadian money should be encouraged to invest at home and foreign capital attracted to promote Canadian industrial expansion.

The more things change the more they stay the same.

Sunday February 18

THEREFORE I say to you, all things for which you pray and ask, believe that you have received them, and they shall be granted you.

Mark 11:24

Monday February 19

FEAR of change causes some persons to be comfortable in their misery, secure in their mediocrity and paralyzed in their prejudice.

William Arthur Ward

Tuesday February 20

M Y daughter Mary makes a type of hot pickles that John really savours. Often when he attends dinners for church functions he will bring along a jar to enjoy with his meal.

At one such dinner he asked the gentleman seated beside him if he would like to have one. Shortly the man's eyes were watering and he was gasping for breath. When he could speak again he said "You know John, many a minister preaches about hell's fire but I swear that you're the first man I ever met who carried samples."

Wednesday February 21

ASH WEDNESDAY

O NCE more the solemn season calls A holy fast to keep.

Thursday February 22

IT was on this day four years ago that my dear sister Sarah married Richard, a longtime friend and neighbour.

For Sarah, it was a first marriage. Richard had been a widower of many years when he and Sarah decided to spend their "golden years" together.

Their wonderful relationship is the type that one reads of in a love story. The happiness that this elderly couple shares is gratifying to see.

I spoke with them both this evening to wish them a happy anniversary and it made me feel so good to hear the joy in their voices.

I'm sure Robert Browning wrote these lines just for Richard and Sarah:

"Grow old along with me! The best is yet to be, the last of life for which the first was made; our times are in his hand who saith 'A whole I planned, youth shows but half; trust God; see all nor be afraid.'"

Friday February 23

ABSENCE sharpens love; presence strengthens it.

Thomas Fuller

Saturday February 24

TODAY I travelled with Marg and Bruce to Brockville, east of Kingston, where Bruce had some business to conclude with a colleague. While Bruce worked, Marg and I decided to do a little sightseeing in the area.

Near Brockville is the little town of Athens—on Highway 42 about 10 kilometres west of Highway 29.

What makes this small town unique is its artwork. On the sides of various buildings on the main street of town are murals celebrating the town's heritage. Financial incentives of $8,000 to $10,000 to attract quality artists were a costly risk. But the first three paintings received rave reviews. By 1993 the main-street gallery had grown to twelve paintings.

One of the most unusual, of the graduating class of 1921, by the well-known artist Dan Sawatsky, has a Model T car that appears to be driving right out of the mural. A painting of a fire that occurred in 1894 graces the side of the fire hall.

My favourite is by artist Lorrie Maruscak, of Athens townspeople on the platform of the old railway station welcoming the daily train, a pastime of many Canadians in every small railway town across the country.

This is a town well worth visiting.

Sunday February 25

WHOEVER believes that Jesus is the Christ is born of God; and whoever loves the Father loves the child born of Him.

By this we know that we love the children of God, when we love God and observe His commandments.

John 5:1–2

Monday February 26

THERE are only two things to aim at in life: first, to get what you want, and, after that, to enjoy it. Only the wisest of mankind achieve the second.

Logan Pearsall Smith

Tuesday February 27

OBLIVION is the dark page, whereon Memory writes her lightbeam characters, and makes them legible; were it all light, nothing could be read there, any more than if it were all darkness.

Thomas Carlyle

Wednesday February 28

A GOOD friend of mine, who lives in the United States, wrote recently to tell me how delighted she is with her new contact lenses.

These are no ordinary lenses—Mary has been legally blind for several years because of a disease called keratonosus. This disease causes the cornea to become thin and irregular, resulting in distortion and progressing quickly to the point where glasses no longer correct it.

Ordinary contact lenses and cornea transplants can help many patients but for Mary they are not suitable.

The Boston Scleral Lens, invented by Dr. Perry Rosenthal of Harvard University is bigger than an ordinary contact lens. It is about the size of a quarter and doesn't make direct contact with the cornea; instead it rests on the sclera, the white tissue of the eye, keeping a layer of artificial tears between the cornea and the lens. The patient puts the tears on the lens before inserting it. Mary says that the lenses are very comfortable, in spite of their size.

The secret to the lens is a special plastic that lets in the oxygen that the cornea needs.

"Edna, I feel as if I have received a miracle! Getting back my sight is the most wonderful thing that I could ever have wished for!"

I am so pleased for Mary and the thousands of others who will benefit from these "miracle lenses."

Thursday February 29

EVERY four years we are given this "bonus" day to enjoy.

I passed my "extra" day at the local school where it was "winter carnival." The children spent the whole day out of doors participating in a wide variety of fun activities.

There was the snowball toss—throwing as many snowballs as possible through a suspended hula hoop.

A snowshoe race was very amusing to watch as the younger children struggled to run with the cumbersome rackets on their feet.

My favourite was the "ski race" where eight children had their feet in harnesses on two 2 x 4 "skis" and they had to "ski" the length of the soccer field. They soon realized that it was an important lesson in cooperation.

Marg and I helped out at the barbecue lunch where we dished up hot dogs and hamburgers to the hungry participants.

It was a delightful way to spend a February day.

March

Friday March 1

SOMETIMES when winter stays too long
And brooks are longing for their song,
There comes a shining silver dawn
When trees of ice put jewels on.

Sparkling before our dazzled eyes,
They hold their beauty like a prize,
And we who look become more wise
While earthly riches shrink in size.

Poor is the man who cannot see
The beauty of such harmony,
The song of sun and sky and tree
Captured in icebound poetry!

My thanks to the unknown author.

Saturday March 2

M ANY people may not be aware that yesterday was an important date in American history. Thirty-five years ago, on March 1, 1965, the
Peace Corps was born.

Founded by then-president John F. Kennedy, it
embraced the concept of people helping people.
Volunteers for the program work abroad with the
people of the country, sharing their know-how
with native farmers, doctors, teachers. The ob-
ject of the program is to assist in raising the level
of the standard of living.

Over the past thirty-five years thousands of men
and women have donated one or two years of their
lives to this worthwhile program. As one young
man said on his return home, "I didn't consider
myself a wealthy young man until I worked in a
country where so many had nothing. The experience will have a profound effect on how I live the
rest of my life."

Many Americans consider the Peace Corps one
of the most significant monuments to the slain
president.

Sunday March 3

ALMIGHTY God, keep us both outwardly in our bodies, and inwardly in our souls that we may be defended from all adversities and all evil.

Book of Common Prayer

Monday March 4

SOONER or later you've heard all your best friends have to say. Then comes the tolerance of real love.

Ned Rorem

Tuesday March 5

As we head into spring Bruce appears to be gearing up for his "here comes spring and I'll bet my clothes don't fit" diet. Last night he turned down second helpings and had just a sliver of homemade pie.

At dinner this evening Bruce steered our conversation towards healthy food and various diet facts.

Some of the interesting (and surprising) things that Bruce has discovered over his years of weight loss efforts may be helpful if you are thinking of losing a few pounds.

Grapefruit does *not* burn body fat.

Foods labeled "made without sugar" may not necessarily be less caloric than those with sugar.

Margarine and butter have the same calories (about 100 per tablespoon) but diet margarine has fewer calories.

Sherbet and ice cream may have the same number of calories. Sherbet has less fat but may have more sugar.

Your stomach does *not* shrink when you diet; you simply become accustomed to eating less food.

Wednesday March 6

A COMPANION loves some agreeable qualities which a man may possess, but a friend loves the man himself.

James Boswell

Thursday March 7

A LEXANDER, Caesar, Charlemagne, and myself founded empires; but on what foundation did we rest the creations of our genius? Upon force. Jesus Christ founded an empire upon love; and at this hour millions of men would die for Him.

Napoleon Bonaparte

Friday March 8

W HY should we think about things that are lovely? Because thinking determines life. It is a common mistake to blame life upon environment. Environment modifies but does not govern life. The soul is stronger than its surroundings.

William James

Saturday March 9

TODAY was a most exciting day for our family. My great-grandchildren Justin and Jenny played their championship hockey game this afternoon and we were cheering spectators at the event.

Jenny and Justin have played hockey for a number of years. Both youngsters are very talented players and excellent skaters so this year they played on a "Rep." team—a team that takes the best players from the area to make a more competitive team than that of the house league.

Phyllis and Bill spent many an hour over the past months driving their children to play games as far away as Owen Sound.

This past two weeks they have been involved in the best-of-seven games championship series with each team winning three games. Today's game was the final and what a match it was.

The score was tied 3–3 with just two minutes remaining when Justin fed Jenny a pass right in front of the net. Jenny banged it home to give her team the win, 4–3.

We were all very excited but I must confess that I was proudest of Jenny when she received her "Most Valuable Player" award and asked the presenter if it could be shared—with the opposition goalie.

I don't think there was a dry eye in the arena.

Sunday March 10

TRULY, truly, I say to you, he who hears My word, and believes Him who sent Me, has eternal life, and does not come into judgement, but has passed out of death into life.

John 5:24

Monday March 11

MY daughter Julia returned recently from a business trip to England. While on these journeys Julia usually tries to do a bit of sightseeing. The following saying was at the entrance to a 12th-century church that she visited.

"You enter this church not as a stranger but as a guest of God. He is your heavenly Father. Come, then, with joy in your hearts and thanks on your lips, offering Him your love and service. Be grateful to the strong and loyal men and women and children who, in the name of God, builded this place to worship, and to all who have beautified it and hallowed it with their prayers and praises. May all who love this house of faith find the inspiration of their labour and rejoice in the power and love of God, that His blessing may rest on you both on your going out and your coming in."

Tuesday March 12

WHAT I admire most in Columbus is not his having discovered a world, but his having gone to search for it on the faith of an opinion.

Wednesday March 13

No barriers, no masses of matter however enormous, can withstand the powers of the mind; the remotest corners yield to them; all things succumb, the very Heaven itself is laid open.

Marcus Manilius

Thursday March 14

IF you will please people, you must please them in their own way; and as you cannot make them what they should be, you must take them as they are.

Lord Chesterfield

Friday March 15

PROBLEMS are opportunities in work clothes.

Henry Kaiser

Saturday March 16

LET me but live my life from year to year,
With forward face and unreluctant soul;
Not hurrying to, nor turning from the goal;
Not mourning for the things that disappear
In the dim past, nor holding back in fear
From what the future veils; but with a whole
And happy heart, that pays its toll
To Youth and Age, and travels on with cheer.

So let the way wind up the hill or down,
O'er the rough or smooth, the journey will be
    joy;
Still seeking what I sought when but a boy,
New friendship, high adventure and a crown,
My heart will keep the courage of the quest,
And hope the road's last turn will be the best.

This poem by Henry Van Dyke is appropriately
titled "Life" and is one of my favourites.

Sunday March 17

GRANT, we beseech thee, Almighty God, that we, who for our evil deeds do worthily deserve to be punished, by the comfort of thy grace may mercifully be relieved; through our Lord and Saviour Jesus Christ.

Collect for the 4th Sunday in Lent.

Book of Common Prayer

Monday March 18

THESE next few lines are in honour of St. Patricks Day, yesterday, the 17th of March. They are part of a very old rune that has survived from the 7th Century and are said to have been spoken by St. Patrick on his way to join in combat with the pagan High King of Ireland.

I arise today
Through the strength of heaven;
Light of sun,
Radiance of moon,
Splendour of fire
Speed of lightning
Swiftness of wind,
Depth of sea,
Stability of earth,
Firmness of rock.

I arise today
Through a mighty strength, the invocation of
    the Trinity,
Through belief in the threeness,
Through the confession of the oneness
Of the Creator of Creation.

Tuesday March 19

D ON'T be afraid to take big steps. You can't cross a chasm in two small jumps.

David Lloyd George

Wednesday March 20

Y OU will do foolish things but do them with enthusiasm.

Colette

Thursday March 21

T ODAY, this first day of spring, our family has two reasons to celebrate. My great-granddaughter Bethany is four years old and her birthday gives us a sense of renewal each year, just as the earth is beginning to show its new life.

Friday March 22

MY dear friend Peggy writes to me from the beautiful Cotswold area in England. Six years ago Peggy did some renovating in her house and changed her home to a "Bed and Breakfast" inn. From her letter, this has been a wonderful change from every aspect.

"I can't tell you how happy I am, Edna. You'll remember that I was very nervous when I first decided to renovate and take on the challenge of running a small inn. Amazingly, everything has gone well right from the start.

I wanted to offer a place to stay in our beautiful area that would allow people who were on a more limited budget to enjoy some time in this historic part of the country.

Senior citizens and young families have been my most-frequent guests.

Now, in this sixth year I find I have many of the same people who were my first guests coming back year after year and for some this will be their sixth year with me.

After John died, I often found myself lonely and unhappy. Not anymore! I enjoy the companionship of my guests and the purpose that the inn has given to my life.

My fondest hope is that you'll visit me very soon."

Saturday March 23

ALL higher motives, ideals, conceptions, sentiments in a man are of no account if they do not come forward to strengthen him for the better discharge of the duties which devolve upon him in the ordinary affairs of life.

Henry Ward Beecher

Sunday March 24

WE beseech thee, Almighty God, mercifully to look upon thy people; that by thy great goodness they may be governed and preserved evermore, both in body and soul; through Jesus Christ our Lord.

Collect for 5th Sunday in Lent.

Book of Common Prayer

Monday March 25

THE need for devotion to something outside ourselves is even more profound than the need for companionship. If we are not to go to pieces or wither away, we must all have some purpose in life; for no man can live for himself alone.

R. Parmenter

Tuesday March 26

THOSE of you who are trivia buffs may find this interesting. On this date in 1855 George Eastman manufactured the first commercial motion picture film.

From his one simple idea came the communications revolution that goes on even today.

Were he alive, I'm sure Mr. Eastman would be astounded to see how his idea has evolved.

Wednesday March 27

ON this day, my dear friend Betty passed away. Betty was an amazing person. She was a shut-in for many years—bedridden for the past several years—yet she was never sorry for herself or unhappy. She was always thinking of others, making items for church bazaars or sending gifts to the neighbourhood children when they celebrated a birthday or a graduation.

Betty's finest quality was her ability to listen to people. She really heard what was said and would give much thought and care before commenting on any issue being discussed.

My heart goes out to her family on this sad day. I, too, shall miss her dearly.

Thursday March 28

IN an effort to give good and comforting answers to the young questioners whom we love, we very often arrive at good and comforting answers for ourselves.

Ruth Goode

Friday March 29

WHEN I left the funeral home after visiting with Betty's family, I remembered the words of Robert Louis Stevenson in his beautiful poem *Consolation*.

He is not dead, this friend; not dead,
But in the path we mortals tread,
Gone some few, trifling steps ahead,
And nearer to the end;
So that you, too, once past that bend,
Shall meet again, as face to face, this friend
You fancy dead.

Saturday March 30

As is often the case at this time of year we decided to begin our spring cleaning.

Isn't it amazing how things accumulate? Each time we do this I feel as if I have gotten rid of everything that is unnecessary only to find that I have boxes more the next time I clean.

What I have enjoyed is finding little treasures that I had completely forgotten about. Today I came across a cranberry mug that was mine as a young child. I used to have my milk in it when we visited at my grandmother's house. I plan to give it to my grandson Marshall for his daughter Bethany.

I guess the nicest thing about cleaning is that each item holds so many fond memories that a day of cleaning becomes a trip down memory lane.

Sunday March 31

PALM SUNDAY

Ride on! ride on in majesty!
Hark! all the tribes hosanna cry
O Saviour meek, pursue Thy road
With palms and scattered garments strowed.

The Book of Common Praise

April

Monday April 1

ALTHOUGH this hymn was written by Rev. H.T. Schenk to celebrate All Saints Day I found it inspiring me to think of many of my friends who really are "saints" here on earth.

Who are these like stars appearing
These before God's throne who stand?
Each a golden crown is wearing
Who are all this glorious band?
Alleluia, hark! they sing
Praising loud their heavenly King.

Who are these in dazzling brightness?
Clothed in God's own righteousness
These, whose robes of purest whiteness
Shall their lustre still possess,
Still untouched by time's rude hand;
Whence come all this glorious band?

These are they who have contended
For their Saviour's honour long
Wrestling on till life was ended,
Following not the sinful throng;
Those who well the fight sustained,
Triumph through the Lamb have gained.

Tuesday April 2

OVER the past few years Marg and I have enjoyed doing Easter crafts with the young ones in our family. This year we decided to try several new ideas that Marg picked up from magazines in the last few weeks.

One of the things that the girls enjoyed most was decorating hats for "Honey Bunnies." Last week Marg and I made the stuffed bunnies. They were very simple—just 1/4 metre of fabric, fiberfill and chenille stems to make the ears stand up was all that was needed for the rabbits.

At the craft store we purchased 2 1/2" diameter straw hats and a variety of tiny flowers and other trim for the hats.

Each of the girls then decorated their bunnies' hats. When they were finished we glued the hats to the bunny heads and they had a "Honey Bunny" to brighten up their rooms.

The boys, not being too keen to decorate hats, chose instead to decorate cookies. Marg made a number of egg-shaped flat sugar cookies and icing in a selection of Easter colours. The boys decorated the cookies in a variety of patterns and they were very pleased with their results. I think what made them happiest was that they were allowed to eat the leftover icing.

Times shared with family give us all the greatest pleasure.

Wednesday April 3

HAPPINESS is not the absence of problems but the ability to deal with them.

Thursday April 4

PERSEVERANCE gives power to weakness, and opens to poverty the world's wealth. It spreads fertility over the barren landscape, and bids the choicest flowers and fruits spring up and flourish in the desert abode of thorns and briars.

S.G. Goodrich

Friday April 5

GOOD FRIDAY

AND Jesus crying out with a loud voice said "Father into Thy hands I commit My spirit." And having said this, He breathed his last.

Luke 23:46

Saturday April 6

IT is by believing, hoping, loving, and doing that man finds joy and peace.

John Lancaster Spalding

Sunday April 7

EASTER SUNDAY

I FIND the Easter Sunday ceremony to be my favourite service in our church. For those of us in the Christian faith it is the basis of our religion—belief in the life to come after death. It was with great hope and joy that I sang this hymn today.

He is risen, He is risen,
Tell it with a joyful voice
He has burst His three day prison,
Let the whole wide world rejoice;
Death is conquered, man is free
Christ has won the victory.

He is risen, He is risen,
He hath opened heaven's gate;
We are free from sin's dark prison
Risen to a holier state;
And a brighter Easter beam
On our longing eyes shall stream.

Monday April 8

As PAST readers know, I am a person who loves to read. I enjoy many types of books but those I like most are mysteries.

John D. MacDonald, Dick Francis and Len Deighton are a few of my favourite authors. Recently I have come to enjoy the works of Dorothy Gilman who has written a number of books where the main character, Mrs. Emily Pollifax, is an elderly white-haired lady. (Is it any wonder that I like her?)

The author of these adventures bases her stories in countries that she has visited.

Mrs. Pollifax on the China Station was set in China as a result of a month-long tour that Miss Gilman enjoyed. Although the opportunity for personal exploring was not a part of her trip, her reaction to China was enthusiastic.

This enthusiasm is quickly felt in her story of Mrs. Pollifax's adventure in the Far East. The characters and the story line are quite believable and as the plot developed I had a lot of trouble putting the book down.

The author divides her time between her house in Portland, Maine and her farm in Nova Scotia. When not busy at a typewriter or tending her flourishing vegetable garden she can be found poring over travel brochures as she plans her (and Mrs. Pollifax's) next adventure.

Tuesday April 9

ANIMALS are such agreeable friends—they ask no questions, they pass no criticisms.

George Eliot

Wednesday April 10

THERE is no truer and more abiding happiness than the knowledge that one is free to go on doing, day after day, the best work one can do, in the kind one likes best, and that this work is absorbed by a steady market and thus supports one's own life. Perfect freedom is reserved for the man who lives by his own work and in that work does what he wants to do.

R.G. Collingwood

Thursday April 11

CONTENT makes poor men rich; discontent makes rich men poor.

Benjamin Franklin

Friday April 12

My friend Lila MacGuiness and I went for a very early walk today. Our journey brought to mind this poem "Dawning" by Margaret Jewell.

I stroll down the lane at daybreak
When the world is still fast asleep,
O'er the hills on the distant horizon
Through the haze the sun starts to creep.

Bursting forth in its golden glory,
Lends a glow to the misty morn.
The air is drenched with the perfume scent
Of a clover field after a rain.

The aroma of wild honeysuckle
Is wafted along on the breeze,
And the woods come alive with music
At the sounds of the birds and the bees.

The dew on the morning grass glistens
Like myriads of sparkling pearls,
And the stirring insects spiral
Up from the earth in swirls.

The tree tops filtering the sun's rays
Give the picture of being enmeshed;
The world awakes from its reverie
To face the dawning refreshed.

Saturday April 13

TODAY Marg and I decided to make our house look like spring. A quick trip to our local supermarket and a little ingenuity was all it took. For several weeks the store has featured floral spring bouquets as well as pots of daffodils, tulips and hyacinths. Until today none of them really fit our budgets but, as luck would have it, nearly all of the flowers had been placed on the "reduced" table and the cost was so minimal that we were able to purchase enough blooms to brighten every room.

Once home we pulled out any of the flowers or greenery that didn't look very fresh. The rest of them we placed in bunches in small bean pots, fruit jars or in glasses inside small baskets.

If you ever need a pick-me-up, check the reduced tables at your local grocery stores. They may have just what you need.

Sunday April 14

AND it came about that while He was blessing them, He parted from them. And they returned to Jerusalem with great joy, and were continually in the temple praising God.

Luke 24:51–53

Monday April 15

A LITTLE more than two years ago the world lost one of its truly funny men with the death, in Mexico, of John Candy.

A Canadian, raised in Toronto's east end, he was a happy, funny student who loved to make people laugh.

In 1969 Candy enrolled in Centennial Community College in Toronto to study journalism and acting. Between classes he worked in the local underground theatre.

In 1971, with fellow Canadian actor Dan Aykroyd, he moved to Chicago where he lived life in the fast lane.

He returned to Toronto in 1974 to star in the hit television series SCTV for which he won two Emmys.

In 1980 Candy began his movie career as policeman Burton Mercer in "The Blues Brothers."

Candy had married his childhood sweetheart, Rosemary, in 1979, and they bought a 20-acre farm in Newmarket where they raised their children.

John Candy had the happy knack of making and keeping friends. In a business where people climb over others to get to the top John made few, if any, enemies.

At his funeral in Brentwood, California longtime friend Eugene Levy said "Feeling his absence will be tremendously hard. Like the air has been sucked out of the world."

His death at 43 has left all of us the poorer.

Tuesday April 16

NOTHING is more important to human happiness than to be part of a fractious, forgiving, warm, tightly-knit family.

Marjorie Holmes

Wednesday April 17

WE ought not to look back unless it is to derive useful lessons from past errors, and the purpose of profiting by dear-bought experience.

George Washington

Thursday April 18

JAKE Frampton related this amusing anecdote to me today.

Jake's friend John has a daughter who is graduating from university this year.

Jake asked if Kelly had decided what to do after graduation.

John replied, "I don't know what her plans are yet but judging from her letters to us, she would make an excellent professional fund raiser."

Friday April 19

OUR Lord has written the promise of the Resurrection, not in books alone, but in every leaf in springtime.

Martin Luther

Saturday April 20

NOTHING can help us face the unknown future with more courage and optimism than remembering the glory moments, and everybody has a few of them.

Eda LeShan

Sunday April 21

TRIBULATION worketh patience; and patience, experience; and experience, hope.

Romans 5:3–4

Monday April 22

MANY years ago I listened to a radio talk show that featured actor Jack Lemmon. He related the best piece of advice that he had ever received. It had come from his father.

Jack had gone to his father, a vice president of a company that made doughnut machines and many varieties of baked goods, to borrow $300 to go to New York to try his hand at acting.

"So you don't want to start in my business. You want to act."

"Yes" answered Jack.

"You love it?"

"Yes! I love it!"

His father handed him the money and said "The day I don't find romance in a loaf of bread I'm going to quit."

What he was saying was that what you do is never as important as loving it.

Tuesday April 23

WE turn not older with years, but newer every day.

Emily Dickinson

Wednesday April 24

SOME of the best shortbread is baked in Scotland. My good friend Mary McConnell says that her great-grandmother used to bake shortbread rounds the size of dinner plates every Christmas and give them to her special friends.

The gift of shortbread symbolized friendship and good luck in Scotland in those days. It may not be the Christmas season but Mary's recipe for shortbread is delicious at any time of year.

2 cups all purpose flour, sifted before measuring
1/2 cup light brown sugar, sifted before measuring
1 cup butter

Preheat oven to 300° F. Cream butter, adding brown sugar gradually. Add flour a few tablespoons at a time. Knead dough on a lightly-floured surface until smooth. Form into a round about the size of a dinner plate on an ungreased cookie sheet. Score lightly with a knife into pre-shaped wedges or roll out the dough and cut with cookie cutters. Bake until golden (about 20–30 minutes for the large rounds.)

Thursday April 25

CHANGE, for the good or for the bad, is not something that I deal with very well. I am a creature of habit and things that upset my routines are not very welcome in my life. I try very hard to be more adaptable but I readily confess that I am not good at it.

Many people have interesting views on change and today I offer just a few.

Change is the law of life. And those who look only at the past or the present are certain to miss the future.

John F. Kennedy

Nothing is permanent but change.

Heraclitus (500 B.C.)

The more things change, the more they remain the same.

Alphonse Karr

Weep not that the world changes—did it keep a stable, changeless state, 'twere cause indeed to weep.

William Cullen Bryant

Observe always that everything is the result of a change, and get used to thinking that there is nothing Nature loves so well as to change existing forms and to make new ones like them.

Marcus Aurelius

The universe is change; our life is what our thoughts make it.

Marcus Aurelius

Friday April 26

WHEN choosing between two evils, I always like to try the one I've never tried before.

Mae West

Saturday April 27

THE harvest of old age is the recollection and abundance of blessings previously secured.

Marcus Tullius Cicero

Sunday April 28

AT the close of life the question will be not, how much have you got, but how much have you given; not how much have you won, but how much have you done; not how much have you saved, but how much have you sacrificed; how much have you loved and served, not how much were you honoured.

Nathan C. Schaeffer

Monday April 29

M Y grandson Fred sent along this amusing list. "You know you're getting older when:

You realize that your first house cost less than the new car you just bought.

You remember when mail was delivered the next day.

You remember when banks didn't look like airline ticket offices.

You remember when movie theatres showed double features and gave away dishes.

You stop worrying about things you can't do anything about."

Tuesday April 30

W E are more often frightened than hurt; our troubles spring more often from fancy than reality.

Seneca

May

Wednesday May 1

You step outside in the early morn,
And there before you new life is born.
There's a feel of excitement just to find
The very first lowly dandelion.
As time goes by they present a pain,
You mow them down, they pop up again.
Kids are amused making chains for hours
And pick them for mom, a bouquet of flowers.
Like a golden carpet, they cover your lawn
Then one fine morning, you find they're gone.
They won't come back for many a day,
They all puffed up and blew away!

Margaret Jewell's poem "Dandelions" seems appropriate for this month when these hardy little weeds really get started.

Most gardeners spend the spring and summer months spraying, pulling, chopping and attacking the yellow pest. I am one of those rare people who finds the dandelion attractive. If it were up to me, dandelions would be a treasured part of everyone's lawn.

Thursday May 2

ONE of the toughest lessons in life is learning to expect the unexpected.

S.H. Dewhurst

Friday May 3

NO life is unimportant. The smallest pebble dropped in the largest lake will still make a ripple.

F. Walsh

Saturday May 4

OUR neighbourhood held a giant garage sale today. About 25 families organized the sale held in the parking lot at the nearby public school. We borrowed tables from the school to display the items to be sold.

The sale was a big success with one minor exception. When Bruce came home with a box of purchases Marg was quick to point out that three of the items that Bruce bought were things that Marg had sold at a sale two years ago.

Sunday May 5

HEREBY know we that we dwell in Him, and He in us, because He hath given us of His Spirit.

John 4:13

Monday May 6

M Y good friends Will and Muriel stopped in today. After a pleasant Saturday's drive Will had an interesting story of one aspect of Ontario's varied history that was unknown to me. It concerned the province's black settlements.

As in the American south, early Ontario settlers accepted slavery as an institution and many wealthy households had slaves.

Although trading in slaves was banned by Britain in 1808, slavery itself continued until 1832 and it wasn't until 3 more decades passed that the U.S. finally abolished the practice.

During this time the abolitionists in the U.S. helped slaves follow the Underground railway to Canada and freedom. Many societies in Ontario sprang up to help escaped slaves establish new lives in the province.

One of these was the Elgin Settlement at Buxton. Founded by William King in 1849, it sold lots of 50 acres at a cost of $2.50 per acre. Houses had to be 18' x 24' and set back 33' from the road. The settlement quickly grew to 2,000 and with the saw and grist mill, potash factory, brickyard, hotel and stores, was considered Ontario's most successful settlement of ex-slaves.

Buxton's black heritage makes it an unusual and fascinating place to visit.

Tuesday May 7

NEIGHBOURS of ours have a young daughter who is a very talented figure skater. They have been approached by several coaches who seem to feel that Michelle is world-champion material. Happily Michelle's parents are realistic and are speaking with a number of experts, including parents of other elite athletes, before they get very excited (or worried) about her athletic future.

Over coffee this morning Pat summarized what she and her husband feel are the most important things that they have learned about having an elite athlete in the family.

"The most important thing" said Pat "is to keep predictions of glory in perspective. Real talent in most sports isn't easily identified before puberty. Growth and development will affect the child's ability in most sports.

"You also must be sure that your child loves her sport and wants to do it. There is a fine line between a supportive parent and one who is pushy. She needs to be motivated by her needs, not ours.

"Choosing a good coach is also a most important task. The coach should be interested in our child as a person not just as an athlete. The coach needs to develop potential while being sure that the sport remains enjoyable.

"Once the family has chosen a coach they need

to leave the job to the coach and not interfere.

"The single most important factor that we've heard is that our child needs to know that we love her for who she is, *not* for what she does or how she performs."

What wise parents.

Wednesday May 8

B RUCE has always claimed that he knew when a storm was coming because he could "feel it in his bones."

Interestingly a study at Stanford University in California revealed that creaking joints may be caused by electromagnetic radiation created by an oncoming storm.

You folks who "feel" the coming of bad weather are apparently on to something.

Thursday May 9

MARSHALL and Jamie brought their two youngsters over to visit this evening.

Four-year-old Bethany is a lovely child and her baby brother Michael, who is seven months old today, is a real going concern. He has learned to crawl and to pull himself up on the furniture.

"He is as excitable and mobile as Bethany was quiet and placid. It's good that Beth came first or we might never have had another one, Gran."

I believe Emerson was speaking for Jamie when he said "There never was a child so lovely but his mother was glad to get him asleep."

Friday May 10

MY friend Marcia, a Bostonian, recently visited the western state of Utah. Marcia spent nearly a week in Salt Lake City where the Mormon Tabernacle is a tribute to the leadership of Brigham Young.

"At the centre of the city is Temple Square. Built on a large city block and surrounded by 12-foot-high walls, it resembles Vatican City.

"Spring comes early to Temple Square. The walls provide wind protection to everything growing inside and the more recently-built tunnels connecting various Mormon buildings warm the soil above.

"By now the flowers and gardens are dramatically beautiful—probably the loveliest city flower display in America.

"Within the walls is the famed 6,500-seat Tabernacle with its wonderful acoustics and an organ that is nearly as famous as the Tabernacle choir.

"As I stood in the back row, Edna, our tour guide dropped a pin on stage. It was perfectly audible.

"This is truly a magnificent city in a beautiful state."

Saturday May 11

THERE is nothing like staying at home for real comfort.

Jane Austen

Sunday May 12

MOTHER'S DAY

WHERE there is love the heart is light,
Where there is love the day is bright,
Where there is love there is a song
To help when things are going wrong....
Where there is love there is a smile
To make all things seem more worthwhile
Where there is love there's quiet peace,
A tranquil place where turmoils cease....
Love changes darkness into light
And makes the heart take "wingless flight"....
And Mothers have a special way
Of filling homes with love each day,
And when the home is filled with love
You'll always find God spoken of,
And when a family, "prays together,"
That family also "stays together"....
And once again a Mother's touch
Can mold and shape and do so much
To make this world a better place
For every colour, creed and race—
For when man walks with God again
There shall be peace on earth for men.

Monday May 13

No man or woman of the humblest sort can really be strong, gentle, pure, and good without the world being better for it, without somebody being helped and comforted by the very existence of that goodness.

Philip Brooks

Tuesday May 14

We are here to help each other, to try to make each other happy.

Saying of the Polar Eskimo

Wednesday May 15

Kind words are the music of the world. They have a power which seems to be beyond natural causes, as though they were some angel's song which had lost its way and come to earth.

Thursday May 16

JAMES Russell Lowell wrote the following lines. To me they are such a beautiful explanation of spring.

Now is the high-tide of the year,
And whatever of life hath ebbed away
Comes flooding back with a ripply cheer
Into every bare inlet and creek and bay,
Now the heart is so full that a drop overfills it,
We are happy now because God wills it;
No matter how barren the past may have been
'Tis enough for us now that the leaves are
    green.

Friday May 17

THIS is the time of year when university students and older high school students are looking for summer jobs.

Recently part-time jobs have been few and far between. My grandson Fred's boys Mickey and Geoffrey have been fortunate in finding work. The past few summers they have helped out on a farm in the area, cleaning stalls, exercising horses and other odd jobs. Before they took the job though, Fred talked with the farmer to be sure that the boys were not going to use any of the farm machinery.

"There are so many serious accidents involving farm machinery. Even men with years of practice can get into difficulty and I certainly didn't want the boys using unfamiliar equipment."

It's certainly wise to check out the safety of our young people's working conditions before an accident happens.

Saturday May 18

THOUGHTS lead on to purposes; purposes go forth in action; actions form habits; habits decide character; and character fixes our destiny.

Tyrone Edwards

Sunday May 19

IF one advances confidently in the direction of his dreams, and endeavours to live the life which he has imagined, he will meet with a success unexpected in common hours.

–Henry David Thoreau

Monday May 20

ALL of this world will soon have passed away. But God will remain, and thou, whatever thou has become, good or bad. Thy deeds now are the seedlings of eternity. Each single act, in each several day, good or bad is a portion of that seed. Each day adds some line, making thee more or less like Him, more or less capable of His love.

Rev. E.B. Pusey

Tuesday May 21

THIS past weekend was the first long weekend of the cottage season. As has been our custom for many years, Marg, Bruce and I spent this time in Muskoka at the summer home of my dear friend Eleanor.

This is the weekend that most cottagers open up after the long winter's closure. As often happens there are some unusual surprises—a cracked pipe, birds nesting in the chimney, to name but a few.

This year it appeared as if nothing untoward had happened at Eleanor's over the winter.

All was going well until Bruce checked down in the boathouse. Eleanor owns one of the old Muskoka launches, built by the Ditchburn boat building family back in the 1920s. It was stored in the boathouse, held up in a sling on chains from the ceiling. Somehow one of the chains had let go, dropping the boat down on its front side. There was considerable damage to both the boat and the decking inside the boathouse.

At first Eleanor was quite upset about the mishap, but after a few phone calls and assurance from the repair man from the Fine Watercraft Restoration Company in the area she was quite philosophical.

"I guess it's like all of us old girls. If we fall down someone picks us up, patches us and sends us on our way."

Wednesday May 22

ONLY when we know what it is to cherish love when sore at some unkindness, to overmaster ourselves when under provocation, to preserve gentleness during trial and unmerited wrong—only then can we know in any degree the "manner of spirit" that was in Christ.

Rev. T.T. Carter

Thursday May 23

SELF-RELIANCE is the greatest gift a parent can give a child.

Friday May 24

TODAY is the birth date of Queen Victoria of England, the late British monarch. One wonders what Victoria would have to say about the state of the monarchy and the royal family. It seems highly possible that we might hear her famous comment "We are not amused" once again.

Saturday May 25

EACH friend represents a world in us, a world possibly not born until they arrive, and it is only by this meeting that a new world is born.

Anaïs Nin

Sunday May 26

WHITSUNDAY

THEREFORE let all the house of Israel know for certain that God has made Him both Lord and Christ—this Jesus whom you crucified.

Acts 2:36

Monday May 27

TALKING is like the harps; there is as much in laying the hand on the strings to stop their vibrations as in twanging them to bring out their music.

Oliver Wendell Holmes, Sr.

Tuesday May 28

THE burden of care-giving to the elderly has become a world-wide problem attracting much attention.

I am one of the very fortunate people in my age category who is very healthy and able to care for myself. I am also lucky that I have been welcomed into my daughter's home. I have my own "apartment" in the house so that we each have our privacy. We are able to be together or alone as we choose. I know that our situation works well for us.

Most of the burden for caring for the elderly, in Canada and around the world, traditionally falls on the shoulders of the women. However, with more and more women entering the workforce, women are faced with a triple burden—holding down a job, running a home and caring for an elderly relative.

Fortunately a growing number of employers are taking the issue of employee family commitments seriously. Many employers are building flex-time into contracts and are providing conferences dealing with work-family conflicts.

As health care costs mount governments are discovering the savings that can be realized by keeping patients in their own homes. But unless the needs of care-givers are identified and addressed, burn-out can happen.

I hope that some solutions can be found to this very difficult problem.

Wednesday May 29

IF you don't have wrinkles, you haven't laughed enough.

Phyllis Diller

Thursday May 30

YOU can never go wrong by following the golden rule: "Do unto others as you would have them do unto you." It is a wonderful adage to live by, always.

Friday May 31

YOU'LL never know what happiness is unless you have something to compare it to. Remember to accept the lows and gain knowledge from them without giving up.

Lee Iacocca

June

Saturday June 1

IT was on this day, oh so many years ago, that my husband George and I were married. We were very young and very much in love as we spoke our vows in the little east-coast church. Today's words of love are a tribute to my husband George and our wonderfully happy life together.

Time flies
Suns rise
And shadows fall.
Let time go by.
Love is forever over all.

Sunday June 2

FORSAKE not an old friend, for the new is not comparable to him. A new friend is as new wine; when it is old thou shalt drink it with pleasure.

The Apocrypha, Ecclesiasticus 8:9

Monday June 3

MY good friends Will and Muriel stopped in for a visit today. Will is a most interesting man to talk with; he has a vast wealth of knowledge on so many topics.

Today Will was telling me about the many and varied types of birds that he has attracted to his garden over the year.

"You know, Edna, it doesn't take much to attract birds. The most effective way, of course, is with a feeder. There are several types, each accommodating different feeding habits. Platform feeders, which act as a beacon to passing birds, are messy but efficient. Roofed tray feeders protect the feed from the elements, while hopper feeders dispense the seed gradually onto the tray.

"Tube feeders are also very popular. They are usually clear plastic with many openings and perches to accommodate several birds at one time.

"Birds like to feed at different heights, so feeder placement is important. Sheltered locations are usually best."

Perhaps these little hints will help you to attract feathered friends.

Tuesday June 4

IF a man has a talent and cannot use it, he has failed. If he has a talent and uses only half of it, he has partly failed. If he has a talent and learns somehow to use the whole of it, he has gloriously succeeded and won a satisfaction and a triumph that few men ever know.

Thomas Wolfe

Wednesday June 5

SOME parents find that by the time their children are fit to live with, they're living with someone else.

Thursday June 6

EXPERIENCE is not what happens to you, it is what you do with what happens to you.

Aldous Huxley

Friday June 7

NEAR shady wall a rose once grew,
Budded and blossomed in God's free light,
Watered and fed by morning dew,
Shedding its sweetness day and night.

As it grew and blossomed fair and tall,
Slowly rising to loftier height,
It came to a crevice in the wall
Through which there shone a beam of light.

Onward it crept with added strength
With never a thought of fear or pride,
It followed the light through the crevice's length
And unfolded itself on the other side.

The light, the dew, the broadening view
Were found the same as they were before,
And it lost itself in beauties new,
Breathing its fragrance more and more.

Shall claim of death cause us to grieve
And make our courage faint and fall?
Nay! Let us faith and hope receive
The rose still grows beyond the wall.

Scattering fragrance far and wide
Just as it did in days of yore,
Just as it did on the other side
Just as it will forevermore.

A.L. Frink

Saturday June 8

THERE is much to be said for living in a small town. My sister Sarah told me this story in her letter today.

"We have new neighbours next door, Edna. They recently moved here from Toronto and are just beginning to get used to 'small town living.'

"Mike needed to rent a tractor mower to cut down the overgrown grass in the back field. He went down to Pouliot's Hardware to rent a machine. Marc, the owner of the store explained to him that the charge for renting the mower was based, not on how many hours he had it out, but on the number of hours the machine was used.

"'How will you know how long I've used it?' Mike wondered.

"Marc looked puzzled and then answered 'Well you'll tell me.'

"Mike found this trust in his honesty the best welcome to town that he could have received."

Sunday June 9

IT is good to give thanks unto the Lord and to sing praises unto thy name, O most high.

Psalm 92:1

Monday June 10

YESTERDAY was my birthday and I was thrilled to be able to celebrate the occasion with many friends and family members.

Have you noticed that it often takes a child to put things in proper perspective? The adults yesterday made many flattering comments.

"My, you don't look your age at all, Edna."

"You look younger every year, my dear."

"Edna, how do you keep your youthful figure?"

My great-grandson Justin brought me back to earth with this: "Wow Gran, if there was even one more candle on this cake you'd probably need a fire extinguisher to blow them out!"

Tuesday June 11

THIS is a time of graduation ceremonies at many universities. Friends of ours attended the graduation of their son from an American university where mortarboards are worn for the ceremony.

A number of the students had printed messages on their caps but Mary's favourite showed ingenuity. The young man had printed:

I Need A Job: Call 234-5678

Wednesday June 12

A NN Landers offered this wise advice: Know yourself. Don't accept your dog's admiration as conclusive evidence that you are wonderful.

Thursday June 13

B E patient with everyone, but above all with yourself. I mean, do not be disturbed because of your imperfections, and always rise up bravely from a fall. I am glad that you make a daily new beginning; there is no better means of progress in the spiritual life than to be continually beginning afresh, and never to think we have done enough.

St. Francis deSales

Friday June 14

H OLDING on to anger is like grasping a hot coal with the intent of throwing it at someone else—you are the one who gets burned.

Buddha

Saturday June 15

Is there anything nicer at this time of year than a delicious barbeque dinner?

Tonight Bruce did one of my very favourites—spareribs. When Bruce cooks ribs they are always so tender and juicy. For any of you that have found spareribs to be dry or tough, I'll pass along Bruce's secret for success.

Preheat your oven to 300°F. Cut meat into sections of about 6–7 ribs. In a pan lined with foil lay the ribs flat and cover each rib section with your favourite barbeque sauce. Seal the ribs in the foil wrap and place in the oven for 2 hours.

Just before serving, remove ribs from foil and place them for about 1 minute on a preheated barbeque.

The results will put you in line for a barbeque "gold medal" from your diners.

Sunday June 16

FATHER'S DAY

Life doesn't come with an instruction book—that's why we have fathers.

Monday June 17

RECENTLY I was lucky enough to enjoy a Blue Jays baseball game at Skydome in Toronto. In fact, I was a guest in a "Skybox," one of the private boxes at Skydome that is owned by a corporation.

Previously, I had attended a game where I sat in the regular seats with my "peanut and cracker-jacks." In the Skybox we snacked on food that would have been welcome at even the most exclusive party. Cheese, crackers, paté, shrimp, and tiny meatballs were just a few of the munchies that we enjoyed. As well, a delightful young lady served drinks or tea or coffee.

Several television sets allowed us to watch replays of the more exciting plays of the game.

It was a pleasant social evening and I enjoyed meeting and talking with the other invited guests of the firm.

I did notice however that watching the game was more difficult—it seemed impolite to say "Oh excuse me, I think that was a Jays hit" in the middle of a conversation.

Seeing the game from a Skybox was probably a once-in-a-lifetime experience and I will remember it always. If you are a baseball fan and this opportunity comes to you, I'm sure that you would enjoy it immensely.

Tuesday June 18

MARSHALL and Bruce played a few holes of golf after work today—yes, golf season is upon us again. This little story is for all of you who enjoy this pastime.

An avid golfer, anxious to get out to the links as quickly as possible, joined a funeral procession, as they drove through red light after red light. Just at the entrance to the club he pulled out of the line. Unfortunately for him there was a motorcycle policeman accompanying the procession. To the golfer's chagrin, the officer made him follow on to the cemetery where he had to remain for the entire service.

Wednesday June 19

A PINCH of probability is worth a pound of perhaps.

James Thurber

Thursday June 20

ALL that mankind has ever learned is nothing more than a single grain of sand that reaches to infinity.

Friday June 21

THERE'S a time each year that we always hold
dear,
Good old summer time;
With the birds and the trees and the sweet
    scented breezes,
Good old summer time,
When your day's work is over then you are in
    clover,
And life is one beautiful rhyme.
No trouble annoying each one is enjoying
The good old summer time.

In the good old summer time,
In the good old summer time,
Strolling through the shady lanes,
With your baby mine;
You hold her hand, she holds yours
And that's a very good sign
That she's your tootsey wootsey
In the good old summer time.

Thanks to Ren Shields for his song of welcome
to the newly arrived season, summer.

Saturday June 22

IF everyone were clothed with integrity, if every heart were just, frank, kindly, the other virtues would be well-nigh useless, since their chief purpose is to make us bear with patience the injustice of our fellows.

Molière

Sunday June 23

AND the work of righteousness shall be peace; and the effect of righteousness, quietness and assurance forever.

Isaiah 32:17

Monday June 24

TODAY is St. Jean Baptiste Day and is a day of great celebration in the province of Quebec. It is a day of parades and speeches and every loyal Quebecois family has a special picnic or dinner to celebrate their patron saint.

Kinsmen of the King divine
Greatest of the prophets line
Blest forerunner of the Lord
Who his praises can record?

Words of praise to St. John the Baptist
by W.E. Enman

Tuesday June 25

CHARM is a way of getting the answer "yes" without asking a clear question.

Albert Camus

Wednesday June 26

As we head into our warm summer many families will enjoy the fine weather camping out in one of our provincial parks. From British Columbia to Newfoundland, vacationers can enjoy the sights and sounds of many diverse terrains.

Many tourists hope to encounter wildlife in their habitats but what many people forget, or choose to ignore, is that these animals are wild. Although some animals in the wild have become accustomed to people, they are not tame and should never be treated as such.

The safest rule of thumb, as suggested by game wardens—do not attempt to pet or feed animals in the wild and *never* try to capture them.

As well, it is wise to know what to do if confronted by a potentially dangerous animal.

To make up for poor eyesight, a bear has keen hearing and an acute sense of smell. If possible, do not surprise a bear and avoid getting between a mother and her cubs. If a bear tries to approach you, move away immediately.

If you should encounter a skunk, give it plenty of room and it will likely wander off. The skunk's foul-smelling spray can burn your eyes and ruin your clothes. If you are sprayed, rinse your eyes with water and wash your clothes with tomato juice.

The porcupine is another animal that needs a

wide berth. They do not throw their quills—you can only be injured by touching them.

If you encounter an animal in the wild, leave it alone.

Thursday June 27

N OT only is a woman's work never done, the definition keeps changing.

Bill Copeland

Friday June 28

W E ought daily or weekly to dedicate a little time to the reckoning up of the virtues of our belongings—wife, children, friends—contemplating them then in a beautiful collection. And we should do so now, that we may not pardon and love in vain and too late, after the beloved one has been taken away from us to a better world.

Jean Paul Richter

Saturday June 29

THE smallest act of kindness is worth more than the grandest intention.

Sunday June 30

As we finish this month I offer a prayer of thanks.

We give the hearty thanks, for the rest of the past night, and for the gift of a new day. Grant that we may so pass its hours in the perfect freedom of thy service, that at eventide we may again give thanks unto thee; through Jesus Christ our Lord. Amen

Book of Common Prayer

July

Monday July 1

CANADA DAY

THIS is the day that we celebrate our wonderful country. Bessie Trull Law's poem "Our Beautiful Land" seems an appropriate tribute to our magnificent homeland.

Happiness is reached in finding
Where the wind and water sing,
Where rugged trails are winding
Through a meadow to a spring;
Rushing from a snow-capped mountain,
Warbling with a passing breeze,
Rippling rhythms toward a fountain
Framed in swaying willow trees.

Far from all the crash and rumble
Of a busy city street,
With our spirits high but humble,
While we stroll at nature's feet,
Feeling music charm and cheer us
Where the heart will understand
That a father's love is near us
In the beauty of our land.

Tuesday July 2

PEOPLE who enjoy working in the garden will probably agree with these words from William Gottlieb. My brother Ben found this wisdom in an old gardening magazine.

"Everything stress is, gardening is not. Stress is hurried and harried; gardening has the pace of nature's season-long rhythms. Stress is feeling powerless and victimized; gardening is control over both your food supply and your immediate environment. Stress is alienation, isolation; gardening is taking part in the great cycles of the earth, the cycles of growth and nourishment, or death and rebirth; it is a daily and joyous ritual of participation in the unity of life. As you garden, you are healed—body and mind, heart and soul."

Wednesday July 3

IT was a perfect evening for a walk so Marg, Bruce and I took full advantage. It was very warm but by following the path of the trail through the woods we were cooled slightly by the light breeze.

Part of the way, past the pond, we stopped just to listen to the quiet. Except for the birds and insect noises, all was still.

I sometimes think that we don't stop to hear the silence nearly enough.

Thursday July 4

THIS is Independence Day for our neighbours to the south. Americans, generally, are much more outgoing and demonstrative in their patriotic displays than we Canadians are.

If you have ever driven through a small American town I'm sure that you've seen the "stars and stripes" hanging on poles at nearly every home. I don't imagine that this overt display makes them any more patriotic than we are, but it surely does make them more colourful.

Happy 220th birthday to you all, kind neighbours.

Friday July 5

ISN'T it funny—when someone else takes a long time doing something, they're slow. When I take a long time to do something, I'm thorough.

Saturday July 6

ONE of the hardest things to realize, specially for the young man, is that our forefathers were living men who really knew something.

Rudyard Kipling

Sunday July 7

INSTRUCT them to do good, to be rich in good works, to be generous and ready to share, storing up for themselves the treasure of a good foundation for the future, so that they may take hold of that which is life indeed.

I Timothy 6:18–19

Monday July 8

I BUMPED into Christie today. She is Phyllis' friend who teaches school.

We paused in our shopping to enjoy a cup of tea and I was interested to hear her comments.

"I'm so glad to be on holiday Mrs. McCann. This was a long and difficult year in my classroom and there were many times that I wondered if I would make it to the summer break.

"Because of enormous financial cutbacks our class numbers are much greater and we seem to be getting more and more needier students each year. Many children arrive at school with less and less general knowledge and little if any understanding of common courtesies.

"Wow! Listen to me go on! Apparently it takes longer to relax and get away from it than it used to, as well."

I don't envy teachers at all.

Tuesday July 9

ONE ship sails East
And another sails West
By the self-same winds that blow.
It's the set of the sails
And not the gales
That determines which way they go.

Wednesday July 10

THIS year the city of Atlanta, Georgia is hosting the summer Olympic Games. Atlanta has been preparing for this great event for years and the athletes can look forward to the best facilities that money can buy.

This year marks the centennial of the modern Olympic games. One hundred years ago in Athens, Greece the modern Olympic era began with 13 nations taking part.

Only the summer Olympic games are being held this year as the winter games return in 1998.

I wish good luck to all of the athletes involved and of course I hope for much success for our Canadian athletes participating.

Citius	Altius	Fortius
Faster	Higher	Stronger

The Olympic Motto

Thursday July 11

Do not be known as a man of success; be known as a man of value.

Albert Einstein

Friday July 12

The philosophy of Glen Cunningham, a great runner of years ago, holds merit today—as it did then.

"My legs are the weakest part of me; I run more from the hips up than the hips down. That is how it has to be with everybody—you go where your heart takes you, not your legs....A handicap can become a great blessing if you keep a strong heart and run like a man, not a jack rabbit."

You see, Glen Cunningham had feet that were partly crippled and without determination he would not have walked, much less run.

Saturday July 13

A SPECIAL birthday wish to my dear friend Marion McDowell who is eighty-one years young today.

"Age only matters when one is aging. Now that I have arrived at a great age, I might just as well be twenty."

Picasso

Sunday July 14

A LL flesh is like grass, and all its glory like the flower of the grass. The grass withers, and the flower falls off, but the word of the Lord abides forever.

I Peter 1:24

Monday July 15

IN these days of recycling it's fun to try to think of new uses for old things. Today Marg, Phyllis and Jamie had a good time with the children's jeans that were outgrown or too worn to wear.

Cutting the legs off the jeans turned them into comfortable and sturdy shorts but what could be done with the leftover legs?

Here are a few ideas that the three came up with.

Sew one end closed and make a casing at the other for rope—you'll have a rough-and-ready tote bag for trips to the beach. The bag could also be used to keep toys that have many "loseable" pieces.

If you split one seam of each leg and sew the legs together you get a larger bag.

Several legs sewn together make a fine pillow cover for when the children want to use a pillow on the floor to watch T.V.

I'm sure that those of you who are ingenious could come up with many more great ideas.

Tuesday July 16

THIS beautiful poem "A Soft Day" seems just perfect for a rainy summer day.

A soft day, thank God!
A wind from the south
With a honeyed mouth;
A scent of drenching leaves,
Briar and beech and lime,
White elder-flower and thyme.

And the soaking grass smells sweet
Crushed by my two bare feet,
While the rain drips,
Drips, drips, drips from the leaves.

A soft day, thank God!
The hills wear a shroud
Of silver cloud;
The web the spider weaves
Is a glittering net;
The woodland path is wet,

And the soaking earth smells sweet,
Under my two bare feet,
And the rain drips,
Drips, drips, drips from the leaves.

Winnifred M. Letts

Wednesday July 17

Summer holidays provide a perfect excuse for those who work to catch up on reading. My daughter Julia is one who will spend days reading book after book and love every minute of it.

"You know, Mom, when I travel I do have time in the evenings when I could read but usually I am so tired or jet lagged that I fall asleep after only two or three pages. Reading the whole book can take so long that I've forgotten how the story started. Having this time free to relax and read is heavenly!"

Thank goodness for our public libraries that can provide us with the very best of reading at no cost.

Thursday July 18

THIS year Marg and I planted a number of fresh herbs in our garden. This small section of plants is giving us many delightful new flavours for old recipes.

Will, our neighbourhood gardening genius, helped us to plant basil, borage, chervil, coriander, dill, sage and thyme. We have concocted some very unusual mixtures with these herbs and many are delicious.

Even if you live in an apartment you can manage a small herb garden at a bright window. Herbs will add much to your cooking.

Friday July 19

COURAGE is the price that life exacts for granting peace. The soul that knows it not, knows no release from little things.

Amelia Earhart Putnam

Saturday July 20

IN Bayfield, north-west of London, Ontario there is a little touch of Holland.

Frank deJong, a descendant of generations of Dutch millers, migrated to Canada after World War II. He bought a parcel of land beside the Bayfield River and set about to recreate his own touch of Holland, a saw and grist mill that would be powered by wind alone.

When it was completed the mill, wind cap and sails of the windmill were a towering 29 metres above the flat marshlands of the river.

The mill is privately owned but visitors are welcomed from May until October.

Trained staff are happy to explain how the four 22-metre wind sails can be positioned to face the wind and rotate to run the saw and grist mill.

This was my first visit to this interesting family business and it was a wonderful experience.

If you are looking for a day's outing, this is a lovely drive.

Sunday July 21

BE gracious to me, O God, be gracious to me, for my soul takes refuge in Thee; and in the shadow of Thy wings I will take refuge, until destruction passes by.

Psalm 57:1

Monday July 22

NO spring, nor summer beauty has such grace, As I have seen in one autumnal face.

John Donne

Tuesday July 23

TODAY is the anniversary of Marg and Bruce's wedding. I can remember as if it were yesterday when Bruce came to us to ask for Marg's hand in marriage. At first we were reluctant to give our blessing because Marg was so young. It was George who reminded me that I was the same age when he and I were married, so argument seemed silly.

When I see today what a happy and successful marriage they enjoy, I can be sure that we were right to bless their union.

Wednesday July 24

A ROAD sign in China when translated reads "Go soothingly on the grassy mud, for therein lurks the skid demon."

Thursday July 25

H OPE is not the conviction that something will turn out well but the certainty that something makes sense, regardless of how it turns out.

Vaclav Havel

Friday July 26

W HEN something goes wrong it is important to talk not about who is to blame, but about who is going to fix it.

Saturday July 27

R ICHES and power are but gifts of blind fate, whereas goodness is the result of one's own merits.

Héloise

Sunday July 28

I REALLY enjoy our summer services at church. Each year when the rector takes his holidays we are treated to the sermons of guest ministers, usually young men and women recently ordained. They bring such a freshness of spirit to their sermons that I come away feeling youthful once again.

As well, this morning we sang one of my favourite hymns, I hope it is one of yours.

Unto the hills around do I lift up
My longing eyes
O whence for me shall my salvation come
From whence arise?
From God the Lord doth come my certain aid
From God the Lord, who heaven and earth
   hath made.

Monday July 29

THE highest pinnacle of the spiritual life is not happy joy in unbroken sunshine, but absolute and undoubting trust in the love of God.

A.W. Thorold

Tuesday July 30

J AKE'S friend John, an avid fisherman, related this story to amuse you today.

A passerby stopped to watch a man fishing on the banks of the river. First he hooked a large trout, but he threw it back. Next he caught an enormous bass, but he threw it back too. Finally he reeled in a small perch that he unhooked and placed in his bag.

The passerby couldn't restrain his curiosity.

"Why did you throw away those beautiful big fish and keep that little one?"

"Small frypan" was the answer.

Wednesday July 31

I T'S hard to imagine that July is ending today. Where do these beautiful days go?

Yellow butterflies
Over the blossoming virgin corn
With pollen-painted faces
Chase one another in brilliant throng

A Hopi Song

August

Thursday August 1

U NDER the towering jackpine trees
The sunlight filters through,
Casting its eerie shadows
On the grasses sparkling with dew.

Like guards in a country churchyard
Proud sentinels they stand,
Ever their constant vigil keep
Over graves on the hallowed land.

The stonework bases have crumbled,
The names long obscured by moss,
Some unknown forgotten resting place
Marked by a worn wooden cross.

Where they blazed a trail to glory,
Those enduring and steadfast pioneers,
The stalwart old trees guard the story
Of those heroes from yesteryears.

Thanks to Margaret Jewell for her tribute to the
Pioneer Cemetery at Big Fork.

Friday August 2

MY brother Ben found himself without cream for a late evening coffee. A quick trip to the local convenience store remedied the situation.

"What time do you close?" Ben asked the clerk on check out.

"Well, we close at eleven—but we start giving dirty looks at about a quarter to."

Saturday August 3

TALK about the joys of the unexpected, can they compare with the joys of the expected, of finding everything delightfully and completely what you knew it was going to be?

Elizabeth Bibesco

Sunday August 4

BE strong, and of a good courage, fear not, nor be afraid...for the Lord thy God, He it is that doth go with thee; He will not fail thee, nor forsake thee.

Deuteronomy 31:6

Monday August 5

I MARVEL at the medical advancements that have occurred during my lifetime. One of the most important breakthroughs has been that of "test-tube" fertilization. For couples previously unable to conceive, it has been nothing short of miraculous.

One of the more interesting aspects of this achievement has been the dramatic increase in the number of multiple births. Triplets, quadruplets, quintuplets and even sextuplets are no longer the rarity they were at the time of the birth of the Dionne Quintuplets.

As well there have been a number of interesting stories develop around the births of these special babies.

In November of 1993 a young mother in Saskatoon had quadruplets—over a period of nine days. After delivery of her first baby labour stopped and it was eight days before baby number two put in an appearance. Again labour stopped and it wasn't until the next day, nine days after the first arrival, that the remaining two babies came into the world.

Birthday parties for the foursome should be interesting.

In England, doctors used a couple's frozen embryos to implant in the woman's womb. Twins were delivered in January 1991.

In 1993 another embryo from the original fertilization was implanted and in July 1994 a baby boy was born. In effect the three children are "time-warp" triplets.

It is truly amazing, is it not?

Tuesday August 6

YESTERDAY'S holiday gave us a chance for a welcome family get together. We gathered at the home of my grandson Fred and his wife June for an old-time summer picnic.

We arrived at about 10 a.m., picnic baskets in hand, and while we unpacked the food to be refrigerated, the children spent time on the tire swings and the slides under the trees.

Fred then announced that they had a number of planned activities for all. For the next few hours we enjoyed a basketball game, races and a sand-sculpturing contest.

I enjoyed the events vicariously from a most comfortable lawn chair in the shade of a large tree.

Lunch was served on picnic tables and we feasted on cold chicken, potato salad and early corn on the cob. Hot biscuits and fruit pies added the finishing touches.

After lunch the children enjoyed a swim in the pond while we adults talked or dozed in the comfort of the lawn chairs.

I can think of no better way to enjoy a holiday than in the company of a loving family.

Wednesday August 7

THE men who try to do something and fail are infinitely better than those who try to do nothing and succeed.

Thursday August 8

THE measure of success is not whether you have a tough problem to deal with, but whether it's the same problem you had last year.

Friday August 9

DURING the summer months many families take advantage of the beautiful weather to see some of our magnificent country.

Travel can be a wonderful experience—except for the many adults and children who suffer from motion sickness, which can take the joy out of travel of any kind.

Experts offer a number of tips that may ease the effects:

While Dramamine is a drug that may offer relief, there are some natural remedies that could prove helpful.

Eating something light before you begin travelling may settle your stomach.

Ground ginger is an old home remedy, so a snack of gingerbread could relieve your symptoms.

When riding in a car sit in the front seat. Seeing where you are going helps. As well, keep fresh air circulating and make frequent stops. Even a few minutes' break can help immensely.

Don't read while the vehicle is moving.

I hope one of these tips may help if you are a sufferer.

Saturday August 10

I ARRIVED in Muskoka early today to visit with my dear friend Eleanor. This beautiful vacation area is truly one of nature's wonders. The rocks, the trees, the sparkling water combine in a beauty that I believe is unrivalled anywhere.

As we enjoyed our tea on the deck this evening I was reminded of the words of John Keats: "A thing of beauty is a joy forever; its loveliness increases, it will never pass into nothingness."

Sunday August 11

THIS morning at the little church at the Kettles we sang one of my favourite hymns.

Now thank we all our God,
With heart and hands and voices,
Who wondrous things has done,
In whom the world rejoices;
Who from our mother's arms
Hath blessed us on our way
With countless gifts of love
And still is ours today.

Monday August 12

HE who sees a need and waits to be asked for help is as unkind as if he had refused it.

Dante

Tuesday August 13

ISN'T it strange that people will say that everything happens for the best but it's always said when something bad happens.

Wednesday August 14

ELEANOR and I spent an enjoyable morning shopping here in Muskoka. The nicest part was being out of doors while we browsed, selected and then paid for our purchases.

Each Wednesday morning during the summer months the Farmers' Market sets up its many and varied booths in Sagamo Park in Gravenhurst. Rain or shine, farmers from the area bring their fruits, vegetables, meats, cheeses and a variety of baked goods to sell to hungry cottagers.

As well, a number of artisans display their wares. You can choose from a vast variety of crafts: hand-knit sweaters, wooden bird houses, hand-crafted jewellery, carved loons and ducks.

We selected our fruits and vegetables for the week and, as well, Eleanor picked out a beautiful sweater and hat set for the newest addition to her family, baby Jessica.

Combining a morning's shopping with the pleasure of being in a beautiful park makes for a pleasant task.

Thursday August 15

ELEANOR and I share a friendship that has spanned decades. We have enjoyed our families' happy times and endured the unendurable together. We have always been there for each other and I cherish her friendship and look on it as one of the great joys of my life. As a tribute to Eleanor I offer the last two verses of Garnett Ann Shultz's poem "My Friend."

You seem to be the helping hand
When troubles come my way,
The stars that light a darkened sky
The dawn at break of day,
You always wear a special smile
So much a joy indeed,
You lend a courage real and sure
In every hour of need.

To me you are the dearest friend
That I have ever known,
No matter what tomorrow sends
I never feel alone,
As faithful as the rising sun
With peace and joy to lend,
I thank God in my every prayer
For giving me my friend.

Friday August 16

TREASURE the love you receive above all. It will survive long after your gold and good health have vanished.

O. Mandino

Saturday August 17

ELEANOR and I enjoyed a beautiful cruise on the lake today. She is so pleased to have the family's antique boat back in the water now that the damage of last winter's mishap has been repaired.

We decided to take a trip up the Indian River to the town of Port Carling. The town is known as the "Hub of the Lakes" for its central position between the three lakes, Muskoka, Rosseau and Joseph.

Port Carling's locks link together Lakes Muskoka and Rosseau and there is a constant parade of boats, both large and small, that use the locks to travel from lake to lake.

The town has a prominent position in Muskoka's boat-building industry, and this heritage is proudly displayed at the Muskoka Lakes Museum. As well, the museum boasts the district's largest collection of native artifacts. Port

Carling was originally a native settlement and still has an Indian village—a native arts and crafts centre situated on the same site.

Steamboat Bay is a unique shopping area right on the water, with plenty of dock space to park the numerous boats that arrive daily.

The town also has a number of stores and restaurants that offer anything you could hope for on a summer's visit.

It was with regret that we left this beautiful little town for our return cruise to the cottage.

Sunday August 18

For the beauty of the earth
For the glorie of the skies
For the love which from our birth
Over and around us lies,
Lord of all to thee we raise
This our sacrifice of praise.

Folliot Pierpont

Monday August 19

ALTHOUGH I enjoyed my stay in Muskoka very much, I am always happy to return home. There is something wonderful about coming back to the place whose comforts are well known to us.

'Mid pleasures and palaces though we may
   roam,
Be it ever so humble there's no place like home.

John Howard Payne

Tuesday August 20

AS we advance in life, we acquire a keener sense of the value of time. Nothing else, indeed, seems of any consequence; and we become misers in this respect.

William Hazlitt

Wednesday August 21

THE Coca-Cola Company ran into an interesting problem when they took their popular soft drink into China.

The company provided merchants with signs printed in English. However, the shopkeepers translated the signs into their own calligraphy and the product became *ke kou ke la*, which means "bite the wax tadpole."

Company researchers eventually came up with a closer calligraphic equivalent: *ko kou ko lo*, which translates roughly to "may the mouth rejoice."

Thursday August 22

HAVE you noticed that the evenings are becoming shorter? Just the last few nights I have been aware that the sun is setting earlier. As well, there has been a little nip in the evening air that portends the autumn to come.

As I walked in the neighbourhood this evening I saw a maple tree whose leaves have already begun to change colour.

Perhaps it's because I love summer so much that these small signs made me feel just a little sad tonight. I could enjoy the warmth of summer until Christmas!

Friday August 23

NOTHING splendid has ever been achieved except by those who dared believe that something inside them was superior to circumstance.

Saturday August 24

IT has been well said that no man ever sank under the burden of the day. It is when tomorrow's burden is added to the burden of today that the weight is more than a man can bear. Never load yourselves so, my friends. If you find yourselves so loaded, at least remember this: it is your own doing, not God's. He begs you to leave the future to Him, and mind the present.

G. MacDonald

Sunday August 25

ALL things are possible to him who believes.

Mark 9:23

Monday August 26

IN the past few years there has been a dramatic rise in the number of cases of asthma. A worldwide surge in pollution has caused air quality to deteriorate. Children seem to be especially vulnerable to poor-quality air—perhaps because the average child breathes in twice as much air per pound of body weight as an adult does.

I have learned much about asthma because Marshall and Jamie's daughter Bethany is an asthma sufferer.

Her first asthma attack occurred about six months ago and it was a very frightening situation to deal with.

Fortunately Jamie recognized that Beth needed help and took her immediately to the hospital. The attending physician used a ventolin mask to ease her breathing discomfort and soon both she and Jamie were feeling better.

Some weeks later Jamie took Beth to an allergist and, at her suggestion, Beth is now using a bronchodilator to give her relief when needed.

As well, Jamie removed the carpeting and other dust collectors from the bedroom. She also replaced Beth's down comforter and feather pillow with those of a synthetic material.

If you should encounter someone who is having a severe attack, call for medical assistance, then try to keep the person calm until help arrives. Keep the person sitting, as it's harder to breathe lying down. These simple procedures may just save a life.

Tuesday August 27

Lord, where we are wrong, make us willing to change; where we are right, make us easy to live with.

Rev. Peter Marshall

Wednesday August 28

Our memory is like a sieve, the holes of which, in time, get larger and larger; the older we get, the quicker anything entrusted to it slips from the memory whereas what was fixed fast to it in early days is still there. The memory of an old man gets clearer and clearer the further it goes back and less clear the nearer it approaches the present time, so that his memory, like his eyes, becomes far-sighted.

Schopenhauer

Thursday August 29

Do not the most moving moments of our lives find us all without words?

Marcel Marceau

Friday August 30

THERE is no good in arguing with the inevitable. The only argument available with an east wind is to put on your overcoat.

James Russell Lowell

Saturday August 31

As this month comes to an end it seems hard to imagine where the time has gone.

I have passed so many interesting and enjoyable days that the summer has simply flown by.

As we look forward to the coming of autumn I hope to have some quiet days where I may relive the joys of summer in my memory.

September

Sunday September 1

SOME years ago when the United Church of Canada was revising its hymn-book, it took a poll of parishioners to determine the most popular hymns.

"In our parish it would be a mighty thin book" announced my husband George.

Only two hymns were selected. One was "Onward Christian Soldiers" and the second one I present for your enjoyment today—"Abide With Me."

Abide with me fast falls the eventide;
The darkness deepens, Lord with me abide,
When other helpers fail, and comforts flee,
Help of the helpless, O abide with me

Hold Thou Thy cross before my closing eyes;
Shine through the gloom and point me to the
   skies
Heaven's morning breaks and earth's vain
   shadows flee
In life, in death, O Lord abide with me.

Monday September 2

LABOUR DAY

EACH Labour Day holiday I like to think of friends who really enjoy their work and are very much suited to their profession.

One of these people is Sam Scott, the dining room hostess at Aston Resort in Muskoka.

Sam is a charming and fascinating lady. She has led an interesting life that many people can only dream of.

Sam was married to a gemologist whose work took them to live in such far-away places as Innuirk, Australia and South Africa.

She and her husband have two children, a son Rob and a daughter Tracey.

After her separation and subsequent divorce, Sam went to work for a well-to-do family, acting as a helper with the children and a travelling companion. Again she was spending time "on the road," as the family had homes in such exotic places as California, Bermuda and several places in Europe.

In speaking with Sam it is easy to see that she has had the marvellous education that only extensive travel can provide.

However, it is her wonderful disposition and her ability to give leadership to the young people working as waiters and waitresses at the resort that make Sam the most beloved of all of the resort's staff.

I salute her on this Labour Day.

Tuesday September 3

For most students in our area this is "back-to-school" day. Marg and I take such pleasure in watching the children in our neighbourhood as they head back to class—some with marked enthusiasm and others with great reluctance.

Teachers have such an awesome responsibility. How they deal with a student may shape that child's life forever.

Today I say a prayer for all teachers.

"May your patience and kindness be an inspiration to all of the young people whose lives you touch. Enjoy this coming year and allow yourself to see all of the good things that you are doing. The results of your work may not manifest themselves until years from now; do not be discouraged. Remember that a smile from you may be the most important thing that happens to a child today. Smile often."

Wednesday September 4

Sometimes the littlest things in life are the hardest to take. You can sit on a mountain more comfortably than on a tack.

Thursday September 5

I HAVE always enjoyed the wit of George Bernard Shaw. The following story is one of my particular favourites.

Shaw was dining in a London restaurant when an orchestra began to play loudly. The music went on for some time until Shaw beckoned the headwaiter and asked "Does the orchestra play requests?"

The headwaiter was delighted to say that they did and asked what the author would like them to play.

"Ask them to play dominoes until I have finished eating" replied Shaw.

Friday September 6

THE fax machine has made a great contribution to the way companies operate. Bruce commented this evening that as a project deadline grew nearer secretaries were kept hopping sending and receiving messages. Corrections, deletions and additions were sent back and forth at an alarming rate.

"Whatever did we do before we had the fax?"

The manager replied dryly, "We did things on time."

Saturday September 7

IF you're not a good example, at least you're a warning.

Sunday September 8

THE grass withers, the flower fades, but the word of God stands forever.

Isaiah 40:8

Monday September 9

As I watched the children walk by on their way to school I was reminded of the poem *Memories Recalled* by Evalena Baker.

Clear and sweet across the country
Rings the village schoolhouse bell,
Calling boys and girls together
From hamlet, hill and dell.

Louder still the bell is ringing
With a strange insistent call,
And the boys and girls are coming
Through the sweet crisp air of fall.

Now the bell has ceased its ringing,
Hurry, hurry, be on time.
School is once more called to order
By the teacher, good and kind.

Soft and low the bell is ringing,
But it rings in memory.
Bringing back as in a vision,
When the school bell rang for me.

Tuesday September 10

WHEN Dr. David See-Chai Lam, the Lieutenant Governor of British Columbia, left his post in 1994 he left behind a glorious reminder of his tenure—22 acres of magnificent gardens.

When Dr. Lam and his wife Dorothy moved into Government House in 1988 they enjoyed walking the grounds. However, along with the many flowers there was an overwhelming and unsightly crop of weeds.

Dr. Lam's first gardening project was weeding and adding walking trails that were opened to visitors.

From the beginning Dr. Lam and his wife carved out a small area for their own garden. They cleared weeds and rubbish and Dorothy planted her vegetable garden.

The next project was an English country garden—"calculated messiness" rather than the formally planted garden.

Dr. Lam realized early that he would need much help. He solicited volunteers from the area and he and his "army" undertook the massive task of planting and restoring the entire gardens.

Queen Elizabeth officially opened the gardens August 18, 1994, the same day that she opened the Commonwealth Games in Victoria.

Dr. Lam explained his love of gardening thus: "When you sow seeds, nourish them, care for them and see them grow, you constantly feel like you're giving life."

Dr. and Mrs. Lam left a wonderful legacy to their beautiful province.

Wednesday September 11

Today's teenagers will have a hard time telling their children what they did without.

Thursday September 12

We could make this world of ours better
We have it at our command,
If instead of pointing a finger,
We would just hold out our hand.

Friday September 13

THIS is the time of year to enjoy our favourite vegetables. Corn, tomatoes, beets and beans are just some of the delicious and plentiful vegetables available to choose from.

I was reading a newspaper article recently that told how health experts rated different vegetables. Each vegetable is rated according to its percentage of 6 nutrients plus fiber content. Vitamin A, vitamin C, calcium, iron, folate and copper are considered in the rankings.

Surprisingly the healthiest vegetable of all is a skinned sweet potato.

Following in order are raw carrots, collard greens, red peppers, kale, dandelions, spinach and broccoli.

At the bottom of the list are garlic, mushrooms, cucumber, alfalfa sprouts and eggplant.

Saturday September 14

THE gardens are at their magnificent best right now. How much I enjoy walking through the neighbourhood and seeing the multicoloured displays.

Peoples' love of beautiful flowers inspired several Canadian health charities to choose three of our favourites to represent their fundraising efforts.

More than four decades ago at a fundraising tea for the Canadian Cancer Society, the tables were decorated with daffodils. When they were used again the following year, it was decided to make these glorious yellow flowers the symbol of the fight against cancer.

Each April about two and a half million daffodils are handed out across the country in exchange for a donation towards research to find a cure for this deadly disease.

In 1985 the Parkinson Foundation adopted a special red tulip as its floral emblem. A Dutch horticulturalist, himself suffering from the disease, which affects muscle control and balance, registered a new variety of tulip. Dr. James Parkinson bulbs, honouring the physician who first diagnosed the disease, are sold across the country in the fall. As well, cut tulips are sold in April with all monies going to aid research.

The carnation is a symbol of hope for those who suffer from Multiple Sclerosis. Each year around Mother's Day the beautifully scented flowers are used to raise awareness and funds for those afflicted with this chronic disease of the nervous system.

Sunday September 15

Trust in the Lord with all your heart, and do not lean on your own understanding. In all your ways acknowledge Him, and He will make your paths straight.

Proverbs 3:5–6

Monday September 16

I found this part of a speech given by James P. Comer very interesting.

"When our youngsters were in elementary school we lived in a community that greatly valued education. When we went to an open house, we had to go very early or we couldn't find a parking place. It was just packed.

"When we went to an open house in a middle school, we didn't have to go early because there were plenty of spaces. When we went to the high school open house, there was an empty parking lot.

"At their point of greatest need in our complex society, we abandon our children."

Copied from a school bulletin.

Tuesday September 17

A FRIEND hears the song in my heart and sings it to me when my memory fails.

Pioneer Girls Leaders Handbook

Wednesday September 18

D O not be troubled because you have not great virtues. God made a million spears of grass where he made one tree. The earth is fringed and carpeted, not with forests, but with grasses. Only have enough of little and common fidelities and you need not mourn because you are neither a hero nor a saint.

Henry Ward Beecher

Thursday September 19

ARE you ever bothered by that annoying light-headed feeling when you stand up suddenly or straighten up after bending down?

According to research, this problem is caused by the sudden change in position. The brain is momentarily left with insufficient blood, which causes the dizziness. We seniors or those who are ill seem especially prone to the condition.

Many people are helped by eating bananas or other potassium-rich foods. Oranges or potatoes (skins on) are high in potassium content and could also help alleviate this irritating problem.

Doctors do suggest, however, that if dizziness persists, you should seek professional advice.

Friday September 20

ARE you looking for a new way to use some of your garden vegetables? Here is a delicious vegetable stew recipe to enjoy.

2 large tablespoons olive oil
1 large onion coarsely chopped
1 bay leaf
2 large sweet green peppers halved, cored, seeded and coarsely chopped
2 medium zucchini (3/4 lb.) cubed

1 clove garlic peeled and minced
4 large tomatoes (2 1/2 lbs.) peeled, seeded and
   chopped
1/2 lb. all purpose potatoes peeled and grated
1 1/2 cups whole corn kernels
1 3/4 teaspoons dried leaf marjoram crumbled
Salt and pepper to taste

Heat olive oil in a large saucepan or Dutch oven over medium heat. Add onion and bay leaf; saute 3–5 minutes or until onion is almost tender. Add sweet pepper, zucchini and garlic; saute 3–5 more minutes or until pepper and zucchini are almost tender.

While the vegetables are cooking, purée half the tomatoes in a blender. Add pureed tomatoes, remaining tomato, potato, corn, salt and pepper to the vegetables in the pot. Bring to a boil; reduce heat to low; cover and simmer 10–15 min. or until potato is tender. Remove bay leaf. Stir in marjoram. Makes 4 servings.

Saturday September 21

TODAY marks the arrival of autumn, the most beautiful of the seasons in our area of the country. Catherine Donnelly writes eloquently of the "Gifts of Autumn."

Autumn came to visit me,
And as she hurried on,
She tripped and spilled her treasures
All over my front lawn.

Golden leaves and ruby ones
Of deepest jewel shades,
Gathered from her wanderings
Over valley, hills and glades.

When I saw Autumn's treasures there
In brilliant disarray,
I quickly stooped and picked them up
And cherished them all day.

Sunday September 22

ST. Peter gave this advice that applies to our lives even these twenty centuries later.

He that will love life,
And see good days,
Let him restrain his tongue
And lips that they speak no guile,
Let him see peace,
And follow after it.

Monday September 23

IF you don't want anyone to know it, don't do it.

Chinese proverb

Tuesday September 24

IN September of 1872 in *My Canadian Journal* Lady Dufferin wrote:

The hills all around, as seen from our celebrated platform (Dufferin Gate, Quebec Citadel) are the most lovely autumn colours, and covered as they are with red and orange trees they really look like flames in the distance, or like gigantic flower gardens; for our trees are quite as brilliant as your best flowers, and if you can imagine your conservatory magnified a million times, and spread over miles and miles of hill and dale, you will begin to understand how we do things in this Canada of ours.

Wednesday September 25

WITH sight, we see. With insight, we understand.

Thursday September 26

Do the young seek absolute truth? Take me along, too. After all, I might have earlier crossed this way, and when you feel as quicksand I might feel as concrete, the path hardened by values I learned when I passed before.

Pearl Bailey

Friday September 27

I LIKE the spring, but it is too young. I like summer, but it is too proud. So I like best of all autumn, because its tone is mellower, its colours are richer, and it is tinged a little with sorrow. Its golden richness speaks not of the innocence of spring, nor of the power of summer, but of the mellowness and kindly wisdom of approaching age. It knows the limitations of life and is content.

Saturday September 28

THE worst ingratitude is gratitude unexpressed.

Sunday September 29

THE Lord will give strength unto His people; the Lord will bless His people with peace.

Psalm 29:11

Monday September 30

BEFORE his retirement my brother Ben had a very wise philosophy. He never brought his work home with him. He showed me a tattered piece of paper that he carried with him always. It read:

"Just for today, when I leave work I will not dwell on how much I did or did not get done. Instead, I will look forward to the evening and be thankful for whatever I accomplished."

October

Tuesday October 1

I ENJOY very much the poetry of Edna St. Vincent Millay. Her work "God's World" seems an appropriate way to start this, the most beautiful month of the year.

O World, I cannot hold thee close enough!
Thy winds, thy wide grey skies!
Thy mists, that roll and rise!
Thy woods, this autumn day, that ache and sag
And all but cry with colour! That gaunt crag
To crush! To lift the lean of that black bluff!
World, World, I cannot get thee close enough!

Lord have I known a glory in it all,
But never knew I this;
Here such a passion is
As stretcheth me apart,—Lord I do fear
Thou'st made the world too beautiful this year;
My soul is all but one of me,—let fall
No burning leaf; prithee, let no bird call.

Wednesday October 2

I ATTENDED a dinner party recently with a number of good friends from my generation. One of our topics of conversation centred around family dinners.

At one time the family ate dinner together every night, except on rare occasions when father may have been away on business. Gradually, as more women joined the workforce and as companies became more global, a "family" dinner became less and less the norm.

As well, children have become involved in organized activities such as hockey, gymnastics, Brownies, Scouts, etc. and these activities often cut into the dinner hour.

Is the "family dinner" a thing of the past? I would like to think not because many of my most treasured memories of my family included those interesting conversations that came about during an ordinary dinner together.

Much insight into the character of each of our girls came at the dinner table. A relaxed and informal time of talking gave each girl a chance to express an opinion or idea important to her.

I can't imagine how a parent would be able to know a child as well if mealtimes were rushed or eaten on a staggered schedule.

Perhaps my friends and I have some old-fashioned ideas but we all felt that family dinners are an important tradition worthy of continuation.

Thursday October 3

A GRANDCHILD is great at making new grand-parents feel both older and younger.

A.L. Sheppard Jr.

Friday October 4

JAMES Michener made these wise comments on travel:

If you reject the food, ignore the customs, fear the religion and avoid the people, you might better stay home. You are a pebble thrown into water; you become wet on the surface but are never a part of the water.

Saturday October 5

WATCH your way then, as a cautious traveller; and don't be gazing at the mountain or the river in the distance and saying "How shall I ever get over them?" but keep to the present little inch that is before you, and accomplish that in the little moment that belongs to it. The mountain and the river can only be passed in the same way; and when you come to them, you will come to the light and strength that belong to them.

M.A. Kelty

Sunday October 6

FOR we know that if the earthly tent which is our house is torn down, we have a building from God, a house not made with hands, eternal in the heavens.

II Corinthians 5:1

Monday October 7

WHILE she was baking Grandma McCann's chocolate cake this weekend Marg came up with a marvellous idea.

She would like to compile a family cookbook, to put together the recipes that have been passed from one generation to the next and that are a form of heirloom.

As we talked about it the idea seemed to get better and better.

"You know Mom, I can call everyone. Aunts, cousins, nieces, nephews, and ask them to give me one or two of their very favourites.

"I think if we're going to put the recipes in a book though, we'll need to test each recipe to be sure that it's accurate.

"If we get Mickey and Geoffrey to help us they could type the recipes on the computer for us."

I also suggested to Marg that it might be fun to include the family tree in the book so that users could see just where the recipe has come from.

I think that this is a marvellous project and one that we'll enjoy very much.

Tuesday October 8

LET us be of good cheer, however, remembering that the misfortunes hardest to bear are those which never come.

James Russell Lowell

Wednesday October 9

This is the harvest
　　that my hands have garnered
Slowly and patiently
　　through the years:

A globe of wisdom
　　plucked from high branches,
A cluster of courage
　　gathered through tears,

Bright berries of laughter
　　tangled with brambles,
Humility gained
　　from the bitterest fruit—

The years have yielded
　　a bountiful harvest,
And tangy and sweet
　　is my hoarded loot.

Grace Noll Crowell

Thursday October 10

As I enjoyed the baseball playoff game on television this evening I had a good laugh.

I was laughing because I was imagining what my dear husband George would say if someone told him that I would be watching baseball on T.V.—and enjoying it!

George was a sports enthusiast to say the least. He enjoyed every sport imaginable and wherever we lived he would support any and all of the local teams.

Often George would talk me into joining him to cheer on whatever group was playing at the time. There was one exception. I did not go to baseball games.

"I'd rather clean cupboards or watch the grass grow" was my rather rude reply to his invitation.

My conversion came about quite slowly. When Toronto was awarded a franchise in the American League I was invited to attend a game at C.N.E. stadium (the Jays' original home). It was a pleasant outing but I was not yet hooked.

When I next attended a game it was at the Skydome and the Jays were in the thick of a pennant race. The enthusiasm of the crowd was infectious and quickly I was cheering and clapping as loudly as anyone.

Soon I was following the team games on both radio and television and a true fan was born.

When George and I meet again, as I know we will, I'll have lots to tell him about "My Jays."

Friday October 11

HOSPITALITY is to be shown even towards an enemy. The tree doth not withdraw its shade, even from the woodcutter.

The Hitopadesa

Saturday October 12

GOD gives to each man, however beset he may be with the world, a few minutes at least daily, when he is utterly alone. I have read Shelley in a Public Lavatory, and learnt Rupert Brookes war sonnets by heart while I was doing my morning duty to this body.

T.P. Cameron Wilson

Sunday October 13

THANKSGIVING SUNDAY

COME ye thankful people, come;
  Raise the song of harvest home!
All is safely gathered in,
Ere the winter storm begin:
God, our Maker doth provide
For our wants to be supplied;
Come to God's own temple, come
Raise the song of harvest home.

Monday October 14

OUR family enjoyed a Thanksgiving dinner yesterday at the home of my grandson Marshall and his wife Jamie. It was a joyous affair with aunts, uncles, cousins and a few family friends sharing the meal.

After yesterday, it was wonderful to have today free to relax and enjoy.

I had planned to spend the day reading until Bruce suggested a drive in the country. I am so glad that I accepted!

Our journey today took us to the lakeside town of Port Dalhousie. This small town on the edge of St. Catharines has long been a fishing town with many fishing boats tied up at the docks edging Lake Ontario.

There are several restaurants that specialize in fish of many types. We enjoyed lunch at "Eddie's Place" a restaurant owned by Eddie Shack, a member of the Toronto Maple Leaf hockey team back in the '60s.

The restaurant overlooks a beautiful park with an enormous carousel. In the summer months the carousel provides hours of pleasure for children and adults alike for only 5 cents a ride.

The trees along the route of our drive were absolutely breathtaking in their colour.

It was a wonderful way to pass a day and I felt truly thankful for my many blessings on this Thanksgiving Monday.

Tuesday October 15

TALK is by far the most accessible of pleasures. It costs nothing in money, is all profit, it completes our education, founds and fosters friendships, and can be enjoyed at any age and in almost any state of health.

Robert Louis Stevenson

Wednesday October 16

As my former readers know I am a letter writer. I write notes and letters very regularly. At first I did much of my writing because I found that long-distance phone calls were simply too expensive for a person on a fixed income. As I wrote more and more I found joy in the writing itself. I spent time thinking of the things that would interest the letter receiver. As well, many of my friends enjoyed getting something in the mail—other than bills—and in turn they began to write me back.

Katherine Stechert Black spoke well of this:

"Even friends I haven't seen in years are still with me, though we no longer sit on one another's kitchen counters on Saturday mornings. The letters and phone calls over the years aren't just biding time till the next visit; sometimes they are the friendship."

Thursday October 17

Some years ago I attended a lecture by Stephen R. Covey, author of the book "The 7 Habits of Highly Effective People."

Mr. Covey was speaking to a group of teachers but what he said could apply to anyone.

"What we are communicates far more eloquently than anything we say or do. There are people we trust because we know their character. Whether they're eloquent or not, whether they have human-relations techniques or not, we trust them and work successfully with them."

Friday October 18

The courage to imagine otherwise is our greatest resource adding colour and suspense to all our life.

Daniel J. Boorstin

Saturday October 19

A SUCCESSFUL man cannot realize how hard an unsuccessful man finds life.

Edgar W. Howe

Sunday October 20

T EACH me to do Thy will; for Thou art my God: Thy spirit is good; lead me into the land of uprightness.

Psalm 143:10

Monday October 21

As the baseball season draws to a close I have a bit of history that I found very interesting.

Have you ever wondered how different teams came up with their names?

The game of baseball as it was first played in the New York area consisted of a field with four posts (bases) in the diamond shape.

One of the teams to enjoy playing in the area was the Brooklyn Excelsiors. By 1884 they were a strong team that toured to cities as far away as Buffalo to show their skills.

In 1886 the team was referred to as the "Brooklyn Bridegrooms" to honour the six members who married during the season.

In the 1890's the team became the "Superbas" but, in fact, their inept play made a mockery of the name.

At the turn of the century, with the arrival of the horse-drawn trolleys, people were constantly having to avoid mishaps by dodging these new-fangled carriages.

Thus was born the "Brooklyn Dodgers" team name—now the "Los Angeles Dodgers."

Tuesday October 22

R EAL learning gets to the heart of what it means to be human. Through learning we re-create ourselves. Through learning we become able to do something we were never able to do. Through learning we reperceive the world and our relationship to it. Through learning we extend our capacity to create, to be part of the generative process of life.

These words from Peter M. Senge in *The Fifth Discipline* really give a definition of what education should be. This is a difficult time for educators and education. With cutbacks in funding, and enormous changes in curriculum, teaching has become an even more arduous task.

It is my fond hope that those who are responsible for educating our children can remember what is truly important and see to it that this generation of learners become a part of the "generative process of life."

Wednesday October 23

IN 1937 when their father was crowned king, six-year-old Margaret asked eleven-year-old Elizabeth whether that meant she would become the next monarch of England.

"Yes" said Elizabeth.

"Poor you," said Margaret.

Thursday October 24

WE are more easily persuaded, in general, by the reasons we ourselves discover than by those which are given to us by others.

Blaise Pascal

Friday October 25

A GOOD slogan for a happy homelife is the old railroad cross-warning sign: "Stop, Look and Listen."

Saturday October 26

M ARGARET, Bruce and I have been enjoying the many and varied recipes that have been coming to us by phone, mail and even by fax, to Bruce's office.

The suggestion of a family recipe book has been enthusiastically received, if the number of recipes sent to us is any indication.

The letters and cards have also been welcome—each one telling a little of when or how the recipe originated.

However, as Bruce aptly put it, "I may be the size of a house before this book is complete."

Sunday October 27

T HOU wilt show me the path of life: in Thy presence is fulness of joy; at Thy right hand there are pleasures for evermore.

Psalm 16:11

Monday October 28

FALLING LEAVES

WHAT are the things I love to see
In autumn when the year grows old?
The black gum leaves of scarlet red;
A hillside poplar turned to gold.

What are the things I love to hear
In autumn when the year is spent?
The wild geese flying overhead,
And drowsy rain with its clean scent.

What are the things I love to smell
In autumn when the year is done?
Blue curling smoke from burning leaves,
And wild grapes purpling in the sun.

Ah, autumn in her passing, leaves
The memory of a lovely song,
And for the heart a legacy
That will last all winter long.

William Arnette Wooford

Tuesday October 29

WHEN we are at variance with someone, the argument we use enables him to see quite well that we wish to win out; that is why he prepares to resist rather than to recognize the truth. So, by beginning this way, instead of making some kind of opening in his mind, we usually close the door of his heart.

On the other hand, how quickly we may open it by gentleness and courtesy.

St. Vincent de Paul

Wednesday October 30

HE that would pass the latter part of life with honour and decency, must, when he is young, consider that he shall one day be old; and remember when he is old that he has once been young. In youth he must lay up knowledge for his support, when his powers of acting shall forsake him; and in age forbear to animadvert with rigour on faults which experience only can correct.

Samuel Johnson

Thursday October 31

Halloween night probably shows best the makeup of a neighbourhood.

Many years ago when Phyllis and Marshall were youngsters, and the family was new to the neighbourhood, it seemed as if every home in the area had at least one child (or more). Halloween saw dozens and dozens of children "shell out."

As the years passed and the children grew older fewer and fewer youngsters would call at the door for treats.

As the young people left for college there were often only a handful of children coming on Halloween night.

Gradually, as the homes became too large for the "empty-nesters," many couples chose to move away. As they moved out, couples with small children looking for more room began moving in.

Tonight we had dozens of children once again, in their Halloween finest, and it was such fun to see how our neighbourhood has become young once again.

November

Friday November 1

WE thank Thee, O God, for the saints of all ages; for those who, in times of darkness, kept the lamp of faith burning; for the great souls who saw visions of large truth and dared to declare it; for the multitude of quiet and gracious souls whose presence has purified and sanctified the world; and for those known and loved by us who have passed from this earthly fellowship into the fuller light of life with Thee. Amen.

Saturday November 2

JAMIE and Marshall have enrolled Beth in the local gymnastics club. From the time she was just walking, Bethany has enjoyed doing somersaults or cartwheels and hanging from the bar on her backyard swing set. Although they are not especially interested in having Bethany pursue a competitive life in gymnastics, both Jamie and Marshall feel that it is important to learn the safe way to indulge in these activities.

Today I accompanied Jamie and Beth to the club for Beth's "Kindergym Hour." I was amazed at the number of children involved at this tender age. About twenty-five youngsters, both boys and girls, were divided into groups of five. Each group had two teenage coaches assisting in a variety of activities. Although I know very little about the sport it was easy to see that the coaches were very skilled and that the exercises and activities had been well designed to deal with very young and undeveloped muscles of the youngsters that they worked with.

It was also a pleasure to note that the children were truly enjoying what they were doing. At the end of the hour Beth came skipping out in her little leotard and cover suit bubbling with enthusiasm.

"Did you see my front roll, Mommy? Amy says it was my best one yet! Isn't that super?"

I hope she'll always be this enthusiastic but I know that should she not want to continue, her parents are wise enough not to push.

Sunday November 3

ONE of my favourite psalms is also one of the shortest, Psalm 117.

Praise the Lord all nations;
Laud him, all peoples!
For his loving kindness is great toward us;
And the truth of the Lord is everlasting.
Praise the Lord.

Monday November 4

THE rung of a ladder was never meant to rest upon, but only to hold a man's foot long enough to enable him to put the other one higher.

Tuesday November 5

THOSE of you who use "Ivory" soap may find this an interesting story.

Many years ago Harley Proctor was manufacturing soap. One afternoon he found that the vat mixing the soap had been left on too long. The mixture was filled with air bubbles but the only "problem" seemed to be that the soap now floated. Delighted with his new-found product Proctor needed to come up with a name. A man who spent many hours reading the Bible, he read Psalm 45:9—"with the smell of myrrh, aloes and cassia: out of the ivory palaces...." hence the name "Ivory" for his new soap.

Wednesday November 6

THE football season is in full swing at this time of year and many wives find themselves serving lunches or dinners on trays in front of the television as their husbands follow their favourite teams. Sometimes wives complain that they are "sports widows" but more and more often these days the women have become just as interested in the games as their husbands.

Some of this interest may come from that old adage "if you can't beat 'em, join 'em" but certainly not all of it.

Possibly another factor in the rising interest is that females are able to participate in the once "male-only" sports. Several U.S. colleges even have female football players. One school that I heard about has a female quarterback and yet another has a girl kicking field goals.

Equality has surely come a long way since my younger days—and we're better for it.

Thursday November 7

THE greatest happiness of life is the conviction that we are loved, loved for ourselves, or rather loved in spite of ourselves.

Friday November 8

SOMETIMES you can't make a person happy. A young lady at a local restaurant was waiting on a stern old lady. In spite of the cheery service the older woman never smiled.

At the meal's end the waitress presented the bill with a happy smile and an "Enjoy your weekend."

"I'm afraid I've made other plans" was the snappy reply.

Saturday November 9

WHEN he was in his mid-80's the great cellist Pablo Casals kept practising his instrument for four or five hours each day. Someone asked him why, at his age, he still worked so hard. "Because," he said "I have a notion that I am making some progress."

Sunday November 10

THE Holy Ghost, proceeding from the Father and the Son, is of one substance, majesty, and glory, with the Father and the Son, very and eternal God.

The Book of Common Prayer

Monday November 11

LET peace be in our prayers, and let peace in all the world come in our time.

A world where no one had to experience war and bear its memories of loss and destruction, as so many of us have had to, would be a wonderful place. Who wants to remember trudging through mud with the deafening explosion of shells overhead? Who wants to recall struggling to comfort a young mother who has just heard she has become a widow? Who among us wants to think of a brother, fiancé, son, or neighbour bidding goodbye for the final time? Let us fervently hope that peace will come to all. Let us pray for all who have fallen in battle.

Tuesday November 12

A GREAT book should leave you with many experiences and slightly exhausted at the end. You live several lives while reading it.

William Styron

One such book that gave me great pleasure was LaVyrle Spencer's *November of the Heart*.

The book, set in Minnesota in 1895, tells the story of Lorna Barnett, a rich man's daughter, who defies her father and the conventions of the times to find true happiness with a boat designer.

November of the Heart is one of a number of "family love stories" written by this prolific author.

The inspiration for this particular novel came from the area in Minnesota where Spencer and her husband of more than thirty years now reside.

LaVyrle Spencer's novels provide us with a gentle sort of tale that only a true believer in romance could write.

Wednesday November 13

To be without some of the things you want is an indispensable part of happiness.

Thursday November 14

A REAL friend is one who helps us to think our noblest thoughts, put forth our best efforts, and to be our best selves.

Friday November 15

A T a time when we now know the dangers of smoking, it was interesting to find that King James I back in 1604 wrote:

"A habit loathsome to the eye, hateful to the nose, harmful to the brain, dangerous to the lungs, and in the black stinking fume thereof, nearest resembling the horrible stygian smoke of the pit that is bottomless."

Saturday November 16

W ILLPOWER is the ability, after you have used three-quarters of a can of paint and finished the job, to close the can and clean the brush instead of painting something that doesn't need it.

Sunday November 17

H E that dwells in the secret place of the most High shall abide under the shadow of the Almighty. I will say of the Lord, He is my refuge and my fortress; my God, in Him will I trust.

Monday November 18

F AITH is an important part of my life. I offer today many thoughts on faith.

Sometimes faith must learn a deeper rest, and trust God's silence when He does not speak.

Faith is the victory that overcomes the world.

Faith is the awareness of utter helplessness without God.

The end of our faith is the salvation of our souls.

The real victory of Faith is to trust God in the dark.

Faith is the eyesight of the soul.

Faith is the substance of things hoped for, the evidence of things not seen.

Tuesday November 19

Isn't it funny how clear a memory of long ago can remain? Here is a time remembered by Lillian Hudson of Toronto.

Back in 1926 Lillian had her first hair perm. Her stepfather, a hairdresser, had promised that she would be the 12-year-old belle of the ball after he took delivery of his magic curling machine from New York.

While Lillian sat under the large metal cap, its electrical cords and chrome cylinders dangling, her dad patiently wound her hair on to the electrodes and saturated it with an ammonia solution.

Because it was his first effort, it took nearly two hours to wind all of the hair onto the electrodes. By this time Lillian was tired and somewhat groggy from the ammonia fumes.

As the switch was flipped to the "on" position, there was a brilliant flash from the machine and all the lights went out.

As it turned out, transformers had been blown all over the Beaches area. Hydro emergency crews told the hairdresser to use only three curlers at a time to avoid more blackouts.

It took a long time but the perm was beautiful, according to Lillian.

Wednesday November 20

H E knows not his own strength that hath not met adversity.

Ben Jonson

Thursday November 21

I F you are anything like me you'll enjoy a good hot bowl of soup on these wretchedly cold damp days. Here is a recipe for a delicious soup— you will need a grocer who stocks watercress year round.

CREAM OF WATERCRESS SOUP

1 cup packed coarsely chopped watercress
3 cups water
3 chicken-flavoured bouillon cubes
2 egg yolks
1/2 cup heavy (whipping) cream
1 tablespoon dry or cooking sherry

In a blender purée watercress and 1/2 cup of water until finely chopped—about 15 seconds.

In a 2-quart saucepan over high heat, heat the watercress mixture, bouillon cubes and the remaining 2 1/2 cups of water to boiling. Reduce heat to low, cover and simmer 10 minutes.

In a small bowl beat egg yolks, cream and sherry. Stir in a small amount of hot soup. Slowly pour the egg mixture back into the soup, stirring rapidly to prevent lumping. Cook, stirring constantly until slightly thickened (do *NOT* boil). Serve hot.

This makes about four 3/4 cup servings.

Friday November 22

Today marks the thirty-third anniversary of the assassination of John F. Kennedy, 35th president of the United States.

One reason that Kennedy was so revered during his time in office was his wife Jacqueline, who was beloved worldwide until her death in 1994.

Strangely enough, the Kennedy family didn't recognize Jackie as the jewel she was until after Jack was elected president. At the time he was running for president the Kennedys felt that Jackie was "too fey" to be involved in the campaign. How they had misjudged her! Even the dazzling Jack sometimes played second fiddle to his beautiful and charming wife during his term as president.

Jacqueline's influence ushered in a time of culture and beauty at the White House and when her young husband was assassinated it was Jackie whose courage and strength held the family together.

As often as we remember that dreadful day in Dallas we will also remember the lovely young mother who was Jacqueline Kennedy.

Saturday November 23

REMEMBER there are no bad days—some are just better than others.

Sunday November 24

O GOD, for as much as without thee we are not able to please thee; Mercifully grant that thy Holy Spirit may in all things direct and rule our hearts, through Jesus Christ our Lord.

Book of Common Prayer

Monday November 25

A MAN and woman should choose each other for life. A long life is barely enough for a man and a woman to understand each other; and to understand is to love. The man who understands one woman is qualified to understand almost everything.

J.B. Yeats

Tuesday November 26

IF you sow kindness you will reap a crop of friends.

Wednesday November 27

AN expert is a person who chooses to be ignorant about many things so that he may know all about one.

E.E. Schattschneider

Thursday November 28

THIS is Thanksgiving Day in the United States and to honour this special day I offer Beryl Stewart's "The Treasured Moment."

A spicy fragrant kitchen,
Gay centerpiece of flowers,
A hearthfire with its crimson flames
Assuring cheerful hours.

A turkey in the oven,
Bright silver on the table,
And children laughing merrily
While Grandpa tells a fable.

Then comes the treasured moment,
The one we all love best,
When hands are folded, heads are bowed
And gratitude expressed.

Friday November 29

FRED gave this advice to his sons Mickey and Geoffrey.

You know you are grown up when:

You are happy when someone else wins the race, the game, the money;

You are more concerned about a friend's happiness than your own;

You can forgive others—and yourself—for human foibles;

You can laugh at yourself and see humour in everyday life.

Saturday November 30

THIS last day of November brought with it the first major snowfall of the season. Although I hate to see the coming of winter I really do enjoy the beauty of the fresh white snow.

After looking at a rather grey and brown month the snow has given a glitter that brightens my spirits as much as it has brightened the ground.

It is pure and beautiful outside—
Within, my room is cozy and warm
A sense of peace with me abides
As I look out at the first snowstorm.

December

Sunday December 1

O N this, the first Sunday of the Advent season, we sang a hymn of welcome for our Lord Jesus. It is a favourite of mine and, I hope, of yours.

O come, O come, Emmanuel,
And ransom captive Israel,
That mourns in lowly exile here
Until the son of God appear
Rejoice! Rejoice! Emmanuel
Shall come to thee, O Israel.

O come, Thou Day-spring, come and cheer
Our spirits by Thine Advent here:
Disperse the gloomy clouds of night,
And death's dark shadows put to flight.
Rejoice! Rejoice! Emmanuel
Shall come to thee, O Israel.

O come, O come, Thou Lord of might,
Who to Thy tribes, from Sinai's height,

In ancient time did give the law
In cloud and majesty, and awe.
Rejoice! Rejoice! Emmanuel
Shall come to thee, O Israel.

(verses 1, 3, 5)

Monday December 2

As the holiday season approaches I look forward to the rituals that are a big part of our family's life together.

The lighting of the advent candles, writing Christmas cards and decorating the house are just a few of the many things that we do with the family.

Pierre Berton spoke of family celebrations this way:

"We celebrate every birthday, we celebrate Easter, Christmas, New Year's Day, Halloween and Valentine's Day, and every other day we can think of. To me, ritual is the glue that keeps society together. Family rituals, like vacations with the whole family, are very important things. To get a sense of community; that is what gives people peace of mind and security."

Tuesday December 3

THE error of youth is to believe that intelligence is a substitute for experience, while the error of age is to believe that experience is a substitute for intelligence.

Wednesday December 4

NOTHING can be truly great which is not right.

Thursday December 5

ONE of the problems facing those of us who are on a fixed income is gift giving at Christmas. What I have found is that sometimes a little ingenuity can go a long way on a budget. Over the years I have come up with some inexpensive but lovely gifts that can be made during these weeks before Christmas.

Plain white paper can be made into beautiful notepaper with just a few pressed flowers glued on. A packet of memo cards may be made up in the same way using recipe file cards and a calligraphy pen.

Inexpensive linen towels become fancy guest towels with an appliqué of your own cross-stitch borders.

If you have saved roses from the summer, it's easy to make your own pot-pourri and place it in your choice of inexpensive but attractive dishes.

For friends who enjoy plants you could buy several small clay pots and paint them in colours to match their decor. As well, old greeting cards or wallpaper could be glued on and varnished to give a more personal touch.

For those of you who knit, hand-knit socks are back in fashion and much appreciated by today's teens. Mittens and hats are always good for the younger children, as are knitted slippers with leather soles, which can be purchased at any craft store.

These gifts take some time but are a real joy to work on—and as they say, it's the thought that counts.

Friday December 6

MARG and I spent a long time at the church today getting ready for tomorrow's Christmas Bazaar. I'm always amazed at how clever our friends and neighbours are—the articles donated to the sale are very often hand-made by the parishioners.

This year's raffle prize is also a poignant reminder of my dear friend Betty. Before she passed away earlier in the year, Betty made a magnificent pine-cone Christmas tree. The tree stands about 2 feet tall, has miniature white light bulbs and is decorated with tiny red bows and garlands of small white beads, all hand strung by Betty.

Almost as if she knew that she might not see this Christmas, the tree was boxed with a card. "Please make sure Edna McCann has this for the Christmas raffle."

I confess that I wiped my eyes frequently as we put her beautiful creation in a place of honour for tomorrow's sale.

Even after her death this selfless soul goes on giving.

Saturday December 7

STRONG hope is a much greater stimulant of life than any single realized joy could be.

Nietzche

Sunday December 8

THIS collect for the second Sunday in Advent comes from the Book of Common Prayer.

Blessed Lord, who has caused all holy scriptures to be written for our learning: Grant that we may in such wise hear them, read, mark, learn and inwardly digest them, that by patience and comfort of thy holy word, we may embrace and ever hold fast the blessed hope of everlasting life, which thou hast given us in our Saviour Jesus Christ. Amen.

Monday December 9

Our bazaar was a huge success! The purpose of the sale is to raise money for those less fortunate than we are. Our parish usually "adopts" a number of families who would not enjoy a happy Christmas without help. The money is used to buy a turkey and other groceries—usually enough for a month—and gifts for the children in the family.

As a remarkable display of love for Betty, the Christmas tree that was raffled made more than fifteen hundred dollars.

Knowing Betty as I did, I feel that she would have found this tribute astonishing. Those of us privileged to know her were not at all surprised.

Tuesday December 10

WHAT a man knows at 50 that he did not know at 20 is, for the most part, incommunicable. The knowledge he has acquired with age is not the knowledge of formulas, or forms of words, but of people, places, actions—a knowledge gained not by words, but by touch, sight, sound victories, failures, sleeplessness, devotion, love— the human experiences and emotions of this earth and of oneself and other men; and perhaps, too, a little faith, a little reverence for things one cannot see.

Adlai Stevenson

Wednesday December 11

SOMETHING that I enjoy very much at this time of year is our senior's bus tour to see the Christmas lights. This evening's ride did not disappoint.

We drove through the lovely town of Oakville tonight and the sight of the stately old homes and tall trees beautifully covered in lights really gave me a sense of the beauty of the coming season.

Any of you who feel the need of a "jump start" into the season have only to take a night drive to see the decorations.

Thursday December 12

ONE ought every day at least, to hear a little song, read a good poem, see a fine picture, and, if possible, to speak a few reasonable words.

Goethe

Friday December 13

MANY people feel that Friday the thirteenth is an unlucky day.

For me this day was a wonderful one. When the mailman arrived, he brought with him an enormous stack of Christmas cards, for Marg and Bruce and for me. I have spent this whole afternoon reading the cards and letters from friends living near and far.

There is nothing that I enjoy more than hearing from friends and this time of year gives us all a chance to keep in touch.

Friday the thirteenth is just another happy day for me and I hope for you.

Saturday December 14

A good memory is fine—but the ability to forget is the true test of greatness.

Sunday December 15

THE Advent of our King
Our prayers must now employ,
And we must hymns of welcome sing
In strains of holy joy.

All glory to the Son
Who comes to set us free
With Father, Spirit, ever One
Through all eternity

Monday December 16

YESTERDAY the young people of our church held a special magic show for the children in the area. It was a wonderful performance with many talented magicians involved in the presentation.

The purpose of the show was to gather tinned and boxed food to go toward our support of less-fortunate families.

The turnout for the show was excellent and the collections far exceeded expectations.

I think that giving to help others is one of the finest lessons that any child can learn. Knowing that anyone, however young they may be, can help, in even a small way, is a lesson in life.

Tuesday December 17

WHEN the Wright Brothers first flew their tiny craft, Kitty Hawk, it was the fulfillment of many people's dreams. For years before their successful flight in 1916, there had been many attempts to fly in man-made crafts. All attempts had met with failure. Can you imagine the feeling of excitement and joy that must have elated, not only Orville and Wilbur, but also everyone whose dream was to soar as the birds.

Great works are performed not by strength but by perseverance.

Johann Wolfgang von Goethe

Self trust is the first secret of success.

Ralph Waldo Emerson

The man who removes a mountain begins by carrying away small stones.

Chinese Proverb

If you wish success in life, make perseverance your bosom friend, experience your wise counselor, conscience your elder brother, and hope your guardian genius.

Joseph Addison

Wednesday December 18

AT this busy time of year it is important to re-member those friends who are shut-ins, or nursing home residents. This can be a very lonely time for the elderly, many of whom have few living friends.

In our area, local high school students have become "guardian angels" for many residents of the nursing home. The young people have been taking the elderly patients across to the mall, both to see the decorated shop windows and to help with any gift purchases. As well, the school choir has come in to the home on several occasions to have carol singing with their aged friends.

One especially nice touch this year is happening tonight. A number of students have prepared a complete Christmas dinner that they will serve in the dining room. Other students have spent this afternoon decorating the tables. Thanks to the generosity of local florists, each guest will receive a poinsettia for their room and these beautiful flowers will add a festive touch to the dinner tables.

John, a senior student, will be Santa Claus for this evening's party. Dressed in his red suit, complete with a padded stomach and false beard he will be presenting a wrapped gift to each resident.

This entire evening was planned and organized by the students themselves. At a time when young people are often criticized for their selfishness, it does my heart good to see such a display of kindness.

Thursday December 19

THERE is great excitement at our home tonight. Bruce has come home with the completed cookbooks that Marg worked so hard to finish for Christmas. The result of her efforts is a bound volume of our family's favourite recipes—a true heirloom that can be handed down to our future generations.

Marg and Bruce intend to give a book to all of the family members who contributed a recipe. As well, there are extra copies for family friends and some to keep for new family members.

This was truly a labour of love for Marg and she is thrilled with the outcome. There is no better feeling than that which comes from a job well done.

Friday December 20

WHEN grace is joined with wrinkles it is adorable. There is an unspeakable dawn in happy old age.

Victor Hugo

Saturday December 21

TODAY we welcome the winter season—with a snowfall. If we must have snow, how nice it is to have it for a "white Christmas."

Sunday December 22

ON this last Sunday before Christmas we enjoyed a number of the beautiful hymns of the season. Here is one of my favourites.

Once in royal David's city
Stood a lowly cattle shed,
Where a mother laid her baby
In a manger for His bed;
Mary was that mother mild,
Jesus Christ her little child.

Monday December 23

MARG and I spent today doing the multitude of last-minute things that are a part of any successful family dinner. I feel confident that we are now completely ready for the large group that will arrive over the next two days.

Marg wisely decided to prepare the vegetables and the many desserts today so that she may also enjoy visiting with the family and not spend all of her time preparing dinner on Christmas day.

Perhaps these lines from Thomas Tusser give us the best advice:

At Christmas play and make good cheer,
For Christmas comes but once a year.

Tuesday December 24

THE beautiful music of the season is a large part of the Christmas Eve service that we will enjoy this evening. Grace Oldershaw's poetic words tell of our love for the carols of Christmas.

When we hear the Christmas carols
How our hearts with gladness beat—
Whether in the quiet churches,
Or in the busy street.

Songs of love and peace and beauty,
Come to us at Christmastide;
Make us kinder to each other,
Plant the seeds of love inside.

So we'll sing our Christmas carols,
With the happy human throng,
Hoping all will find a blessing
In the music of a song.

Wednesday December 25

CHRISTMAS DAY

MAY I wish to you all a very merry Christmas! On this happy day I hope that you will enjoy the fellowship and love of family and friends wherever you may be.

Happy, happy Christmas that can win us back to the delusions of our childish days; that can recall to the old man the pleasures of his youth; that can transport the sailor and the traveller, thousands of miles away, back to his own fireside and his quiet home!

Charles Dickens

Thursday December 26

"BOXING Day," which we celebrate here in Canada, is a part of our British heritage. The name came from the tradition of sending Christmas boxes to errand boys, porters, postmen, and others to whom a show of appreciation was given.

I still laugh when I think of my friend Roger's reaction to my explanation of "Boxing Day." Roger, an American, had his own idea:

"Edna, I thought that 'Boxing Day' meant that fathers looked for the biggest box available and crawled in to find a quiet resting spot after the excitement of the day before."

Friday December 27

You will find as you look back upon your life that the moments when you have really lived are the moments when you have done things in the spirit of love.

Henry Drummond

Saturday December 28

The evening of a well-spent life brings its lamp with it.

Sunday December 29

O God, who makest us glad with the yearly re-membrance of the birth of thy only Son Jesus Christ: Grant that as we joyfully receive him as our Redeemer, we may with sure confidence behold him when he shall come again to be our Judge; who liveth and reigneth with thee and the Holy Ghost now and ever. Amen.

The Book of Common Prayer

Monday December 30

CHILDREN have the most delightful ways of keeping us young—or at least young at heart.

In our family it is a tradition that the children are responsible for selecting their Christmas gifts for the adults—aunts, uncles, grandparents etc. receive a gift that has been chosen by the child alone—no adult help allowed!

The children learn early to find out what interests the gift recipient and to choose carefully from their limited budgets.

Justin and Jenny surprised me with two beautiful books of quotations that they found in a local book store.

"Maybe you can find something for your book, Gran."

Obviously they have learned well to put thought into their gift giving.

Tuesday December 31

A GAIN we look to the year just past and ahead to the new year that comes to us tomorrow.
We can change nothing of that which is now past but we have a marvellous chance to use this coming year in the best ways possible.

This is the time of endings,
but of new beginnings, too.
God sends me another year
and maketh all things new.
Another hope, another chance,
another road to take.
Another star to follow,
and another start to make.

My best wishes to you all for a happy and healthy New Year.